Fashion Sketches

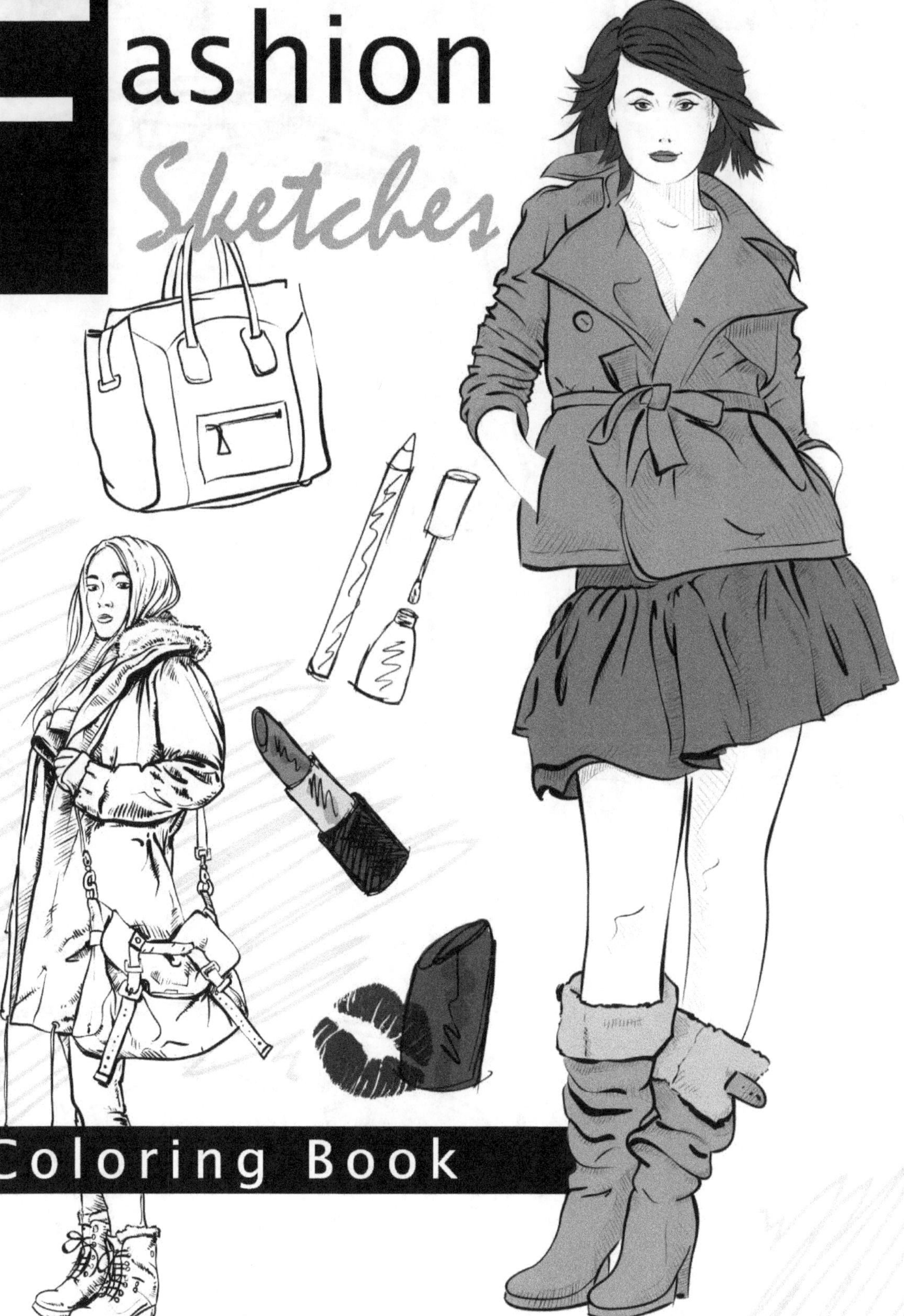

Coloring Book

COLOR TEST PAGE

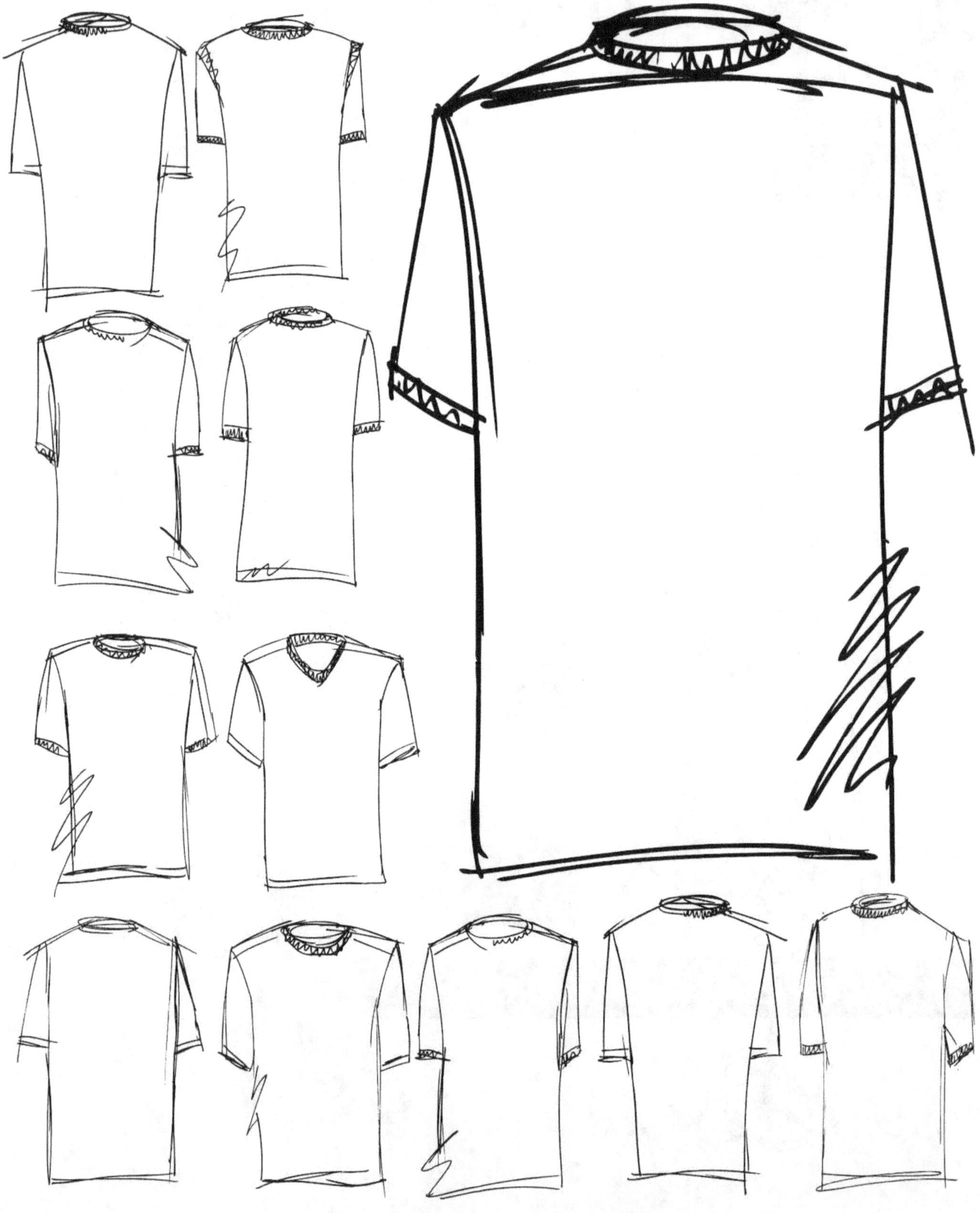

COLOR TEST PAGE

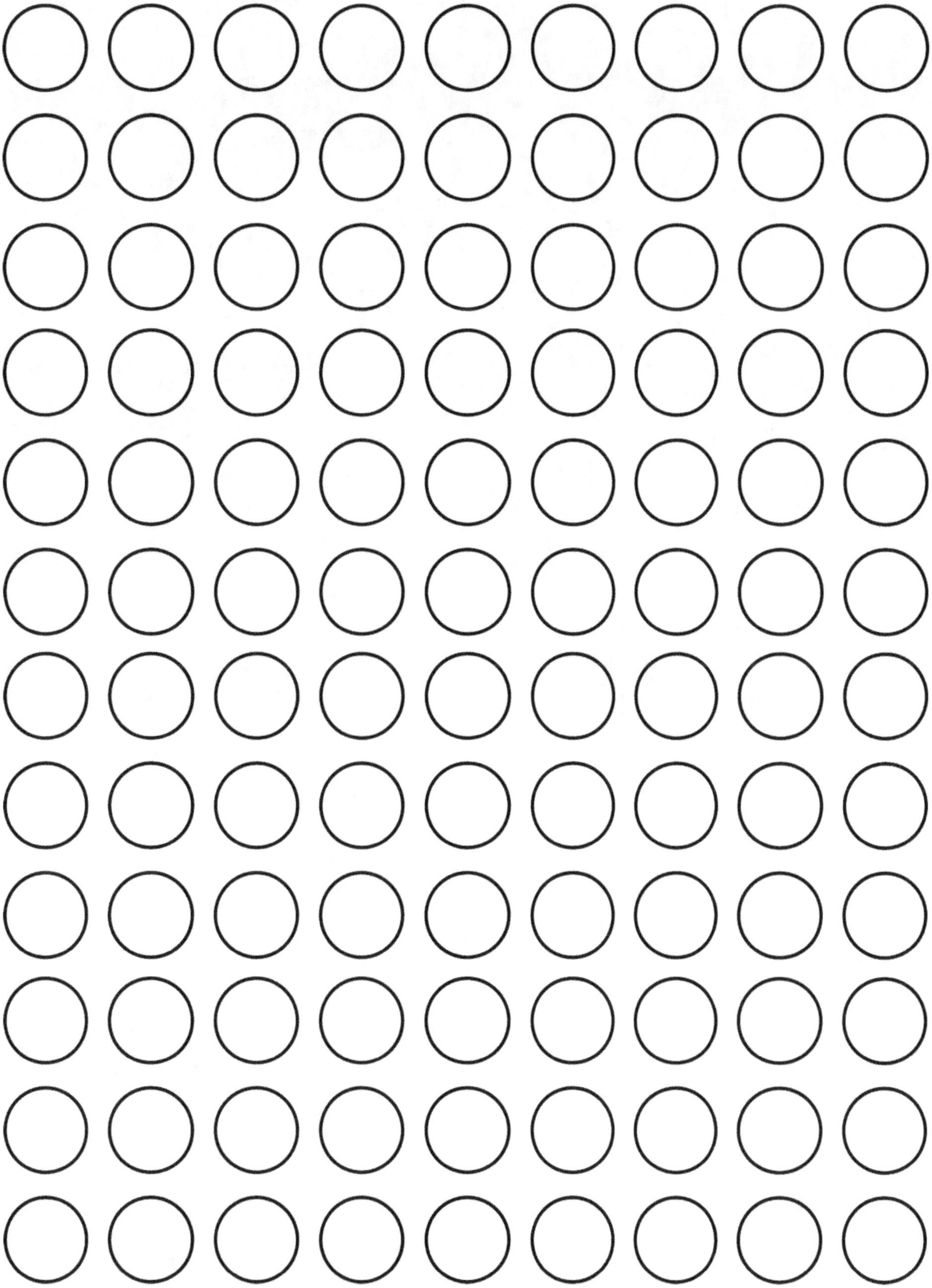

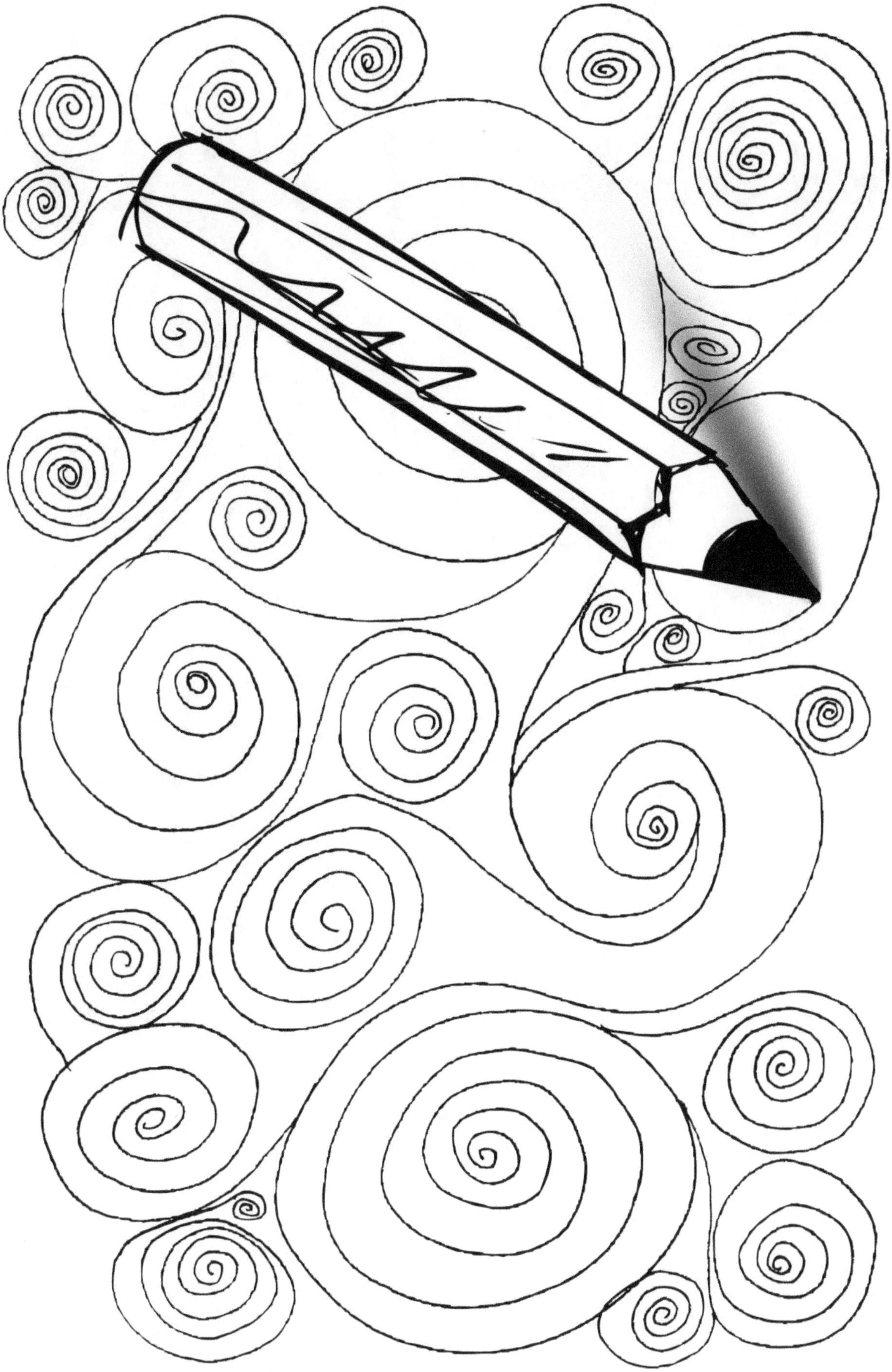

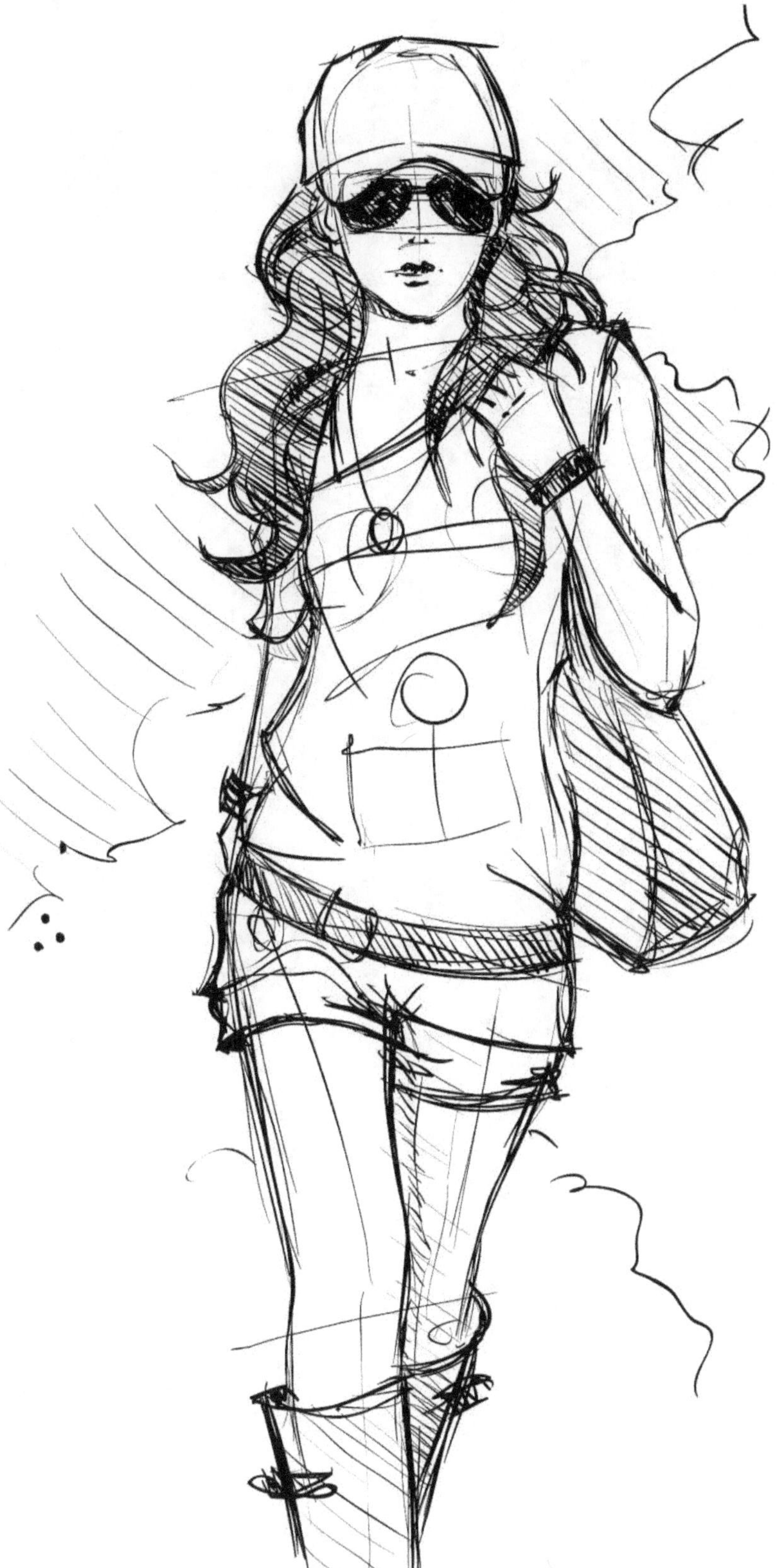

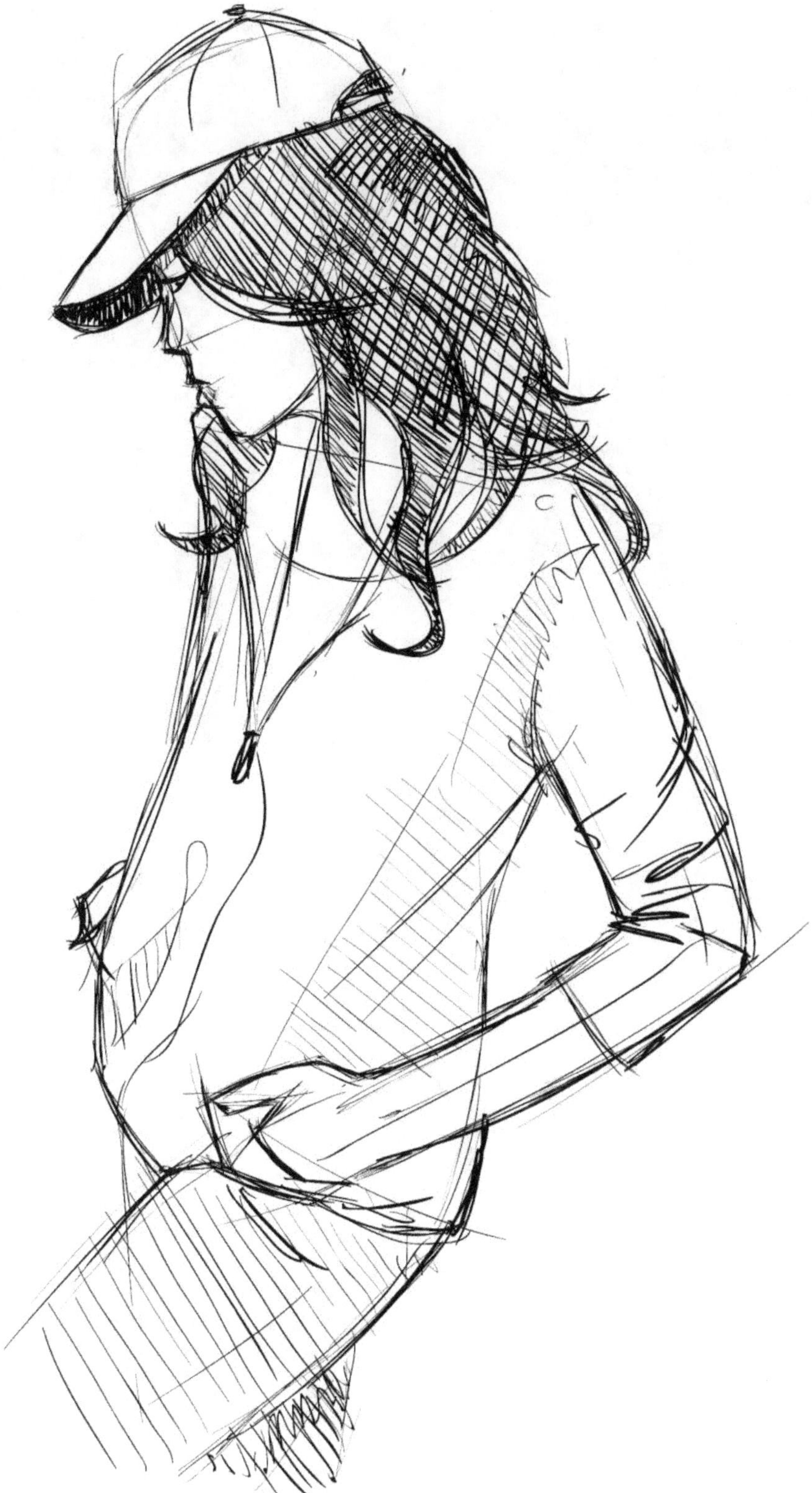

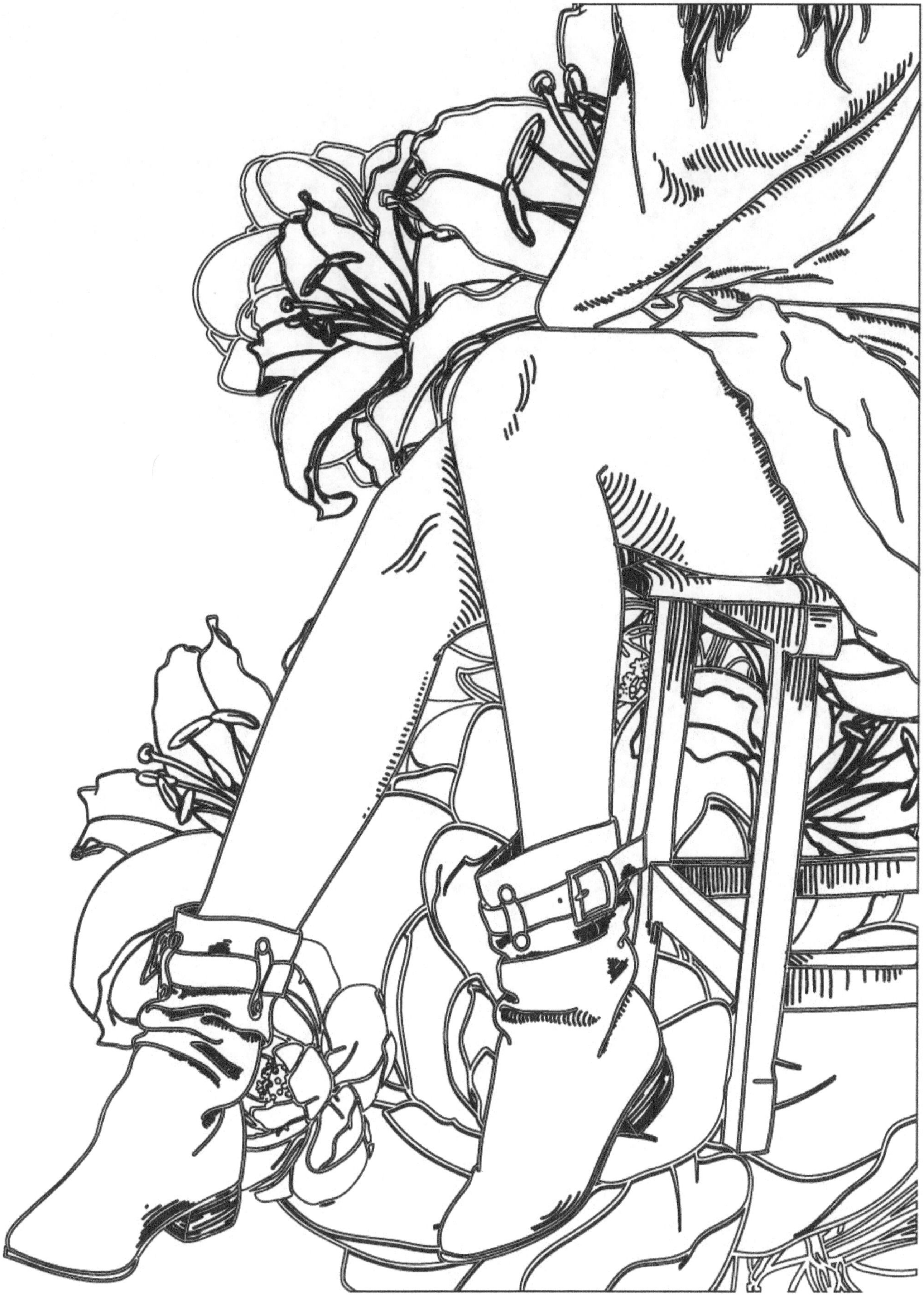

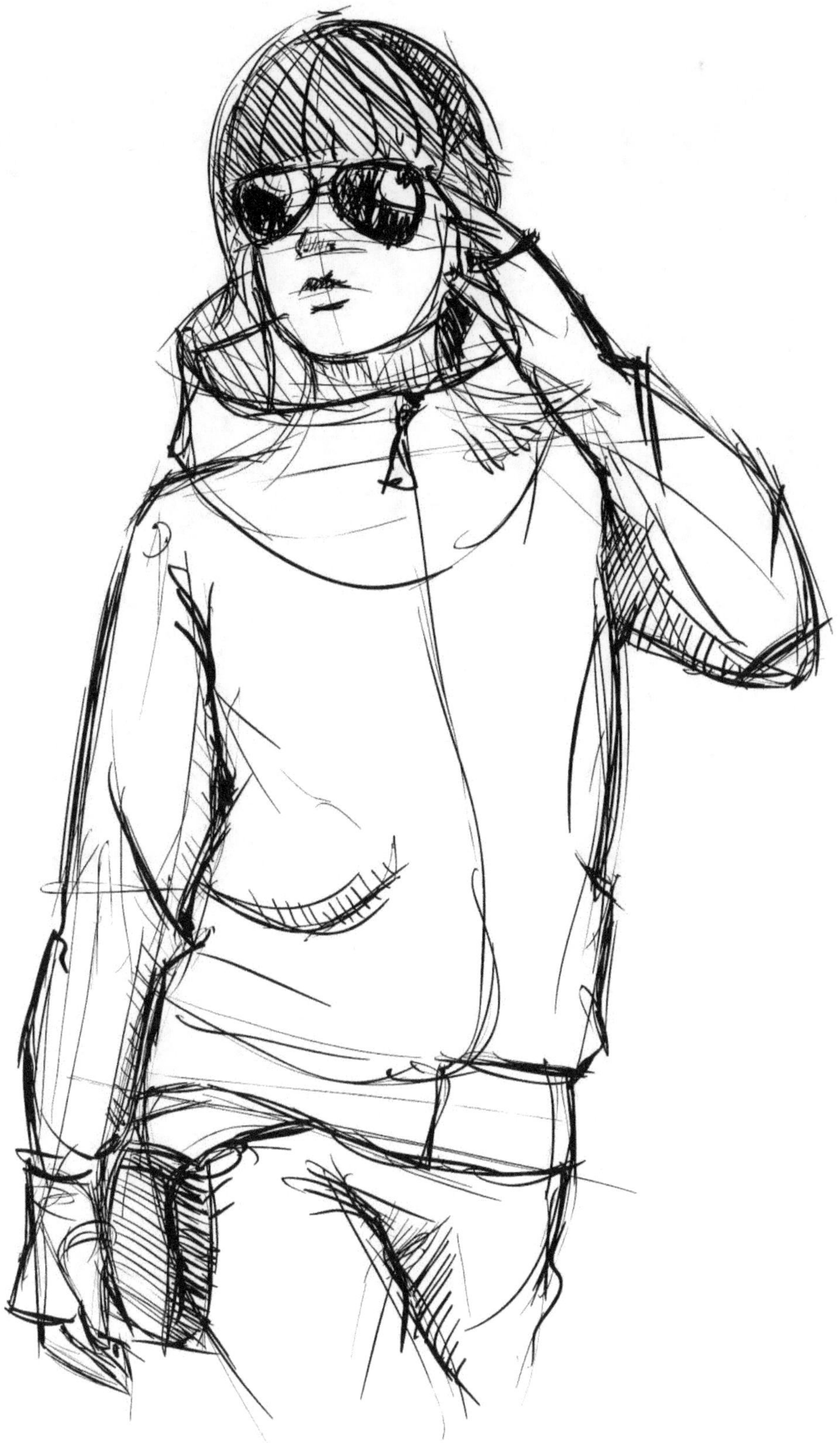

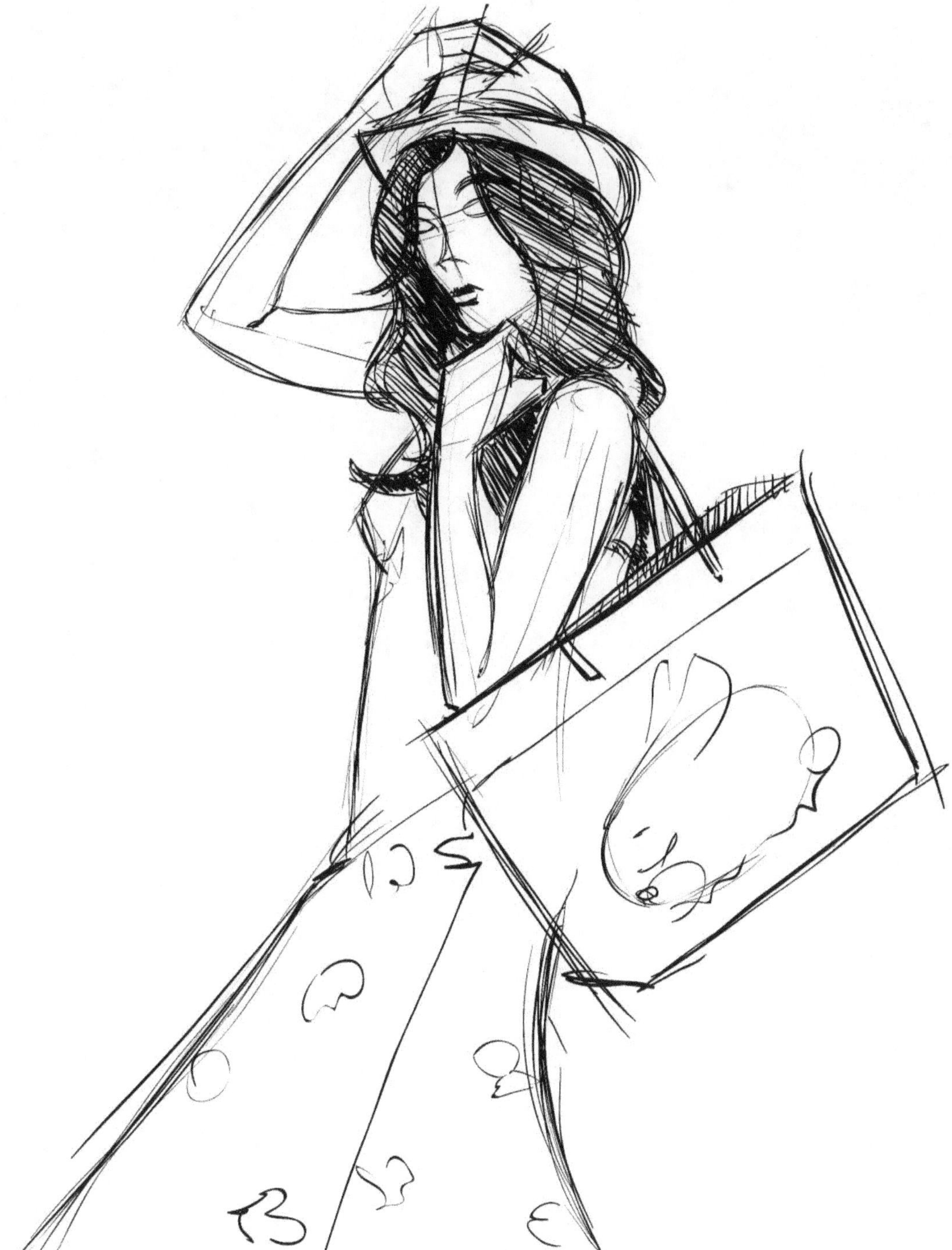

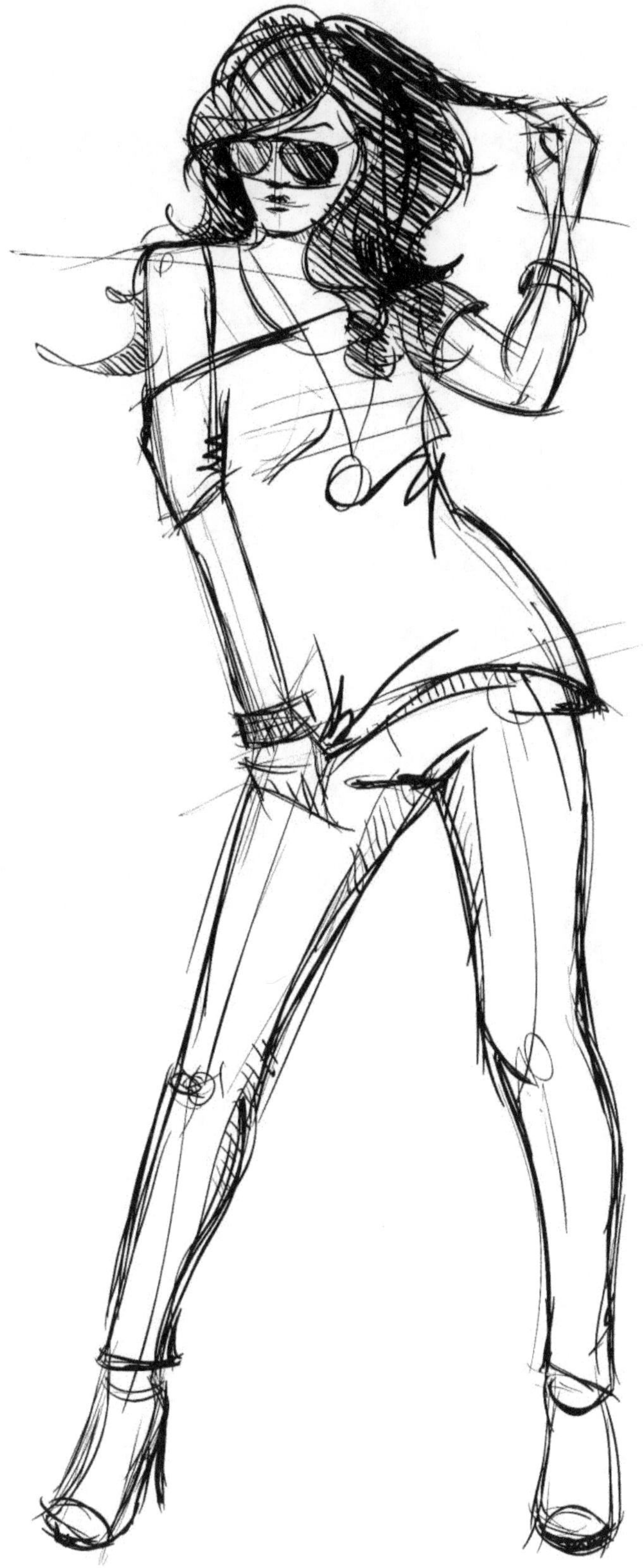

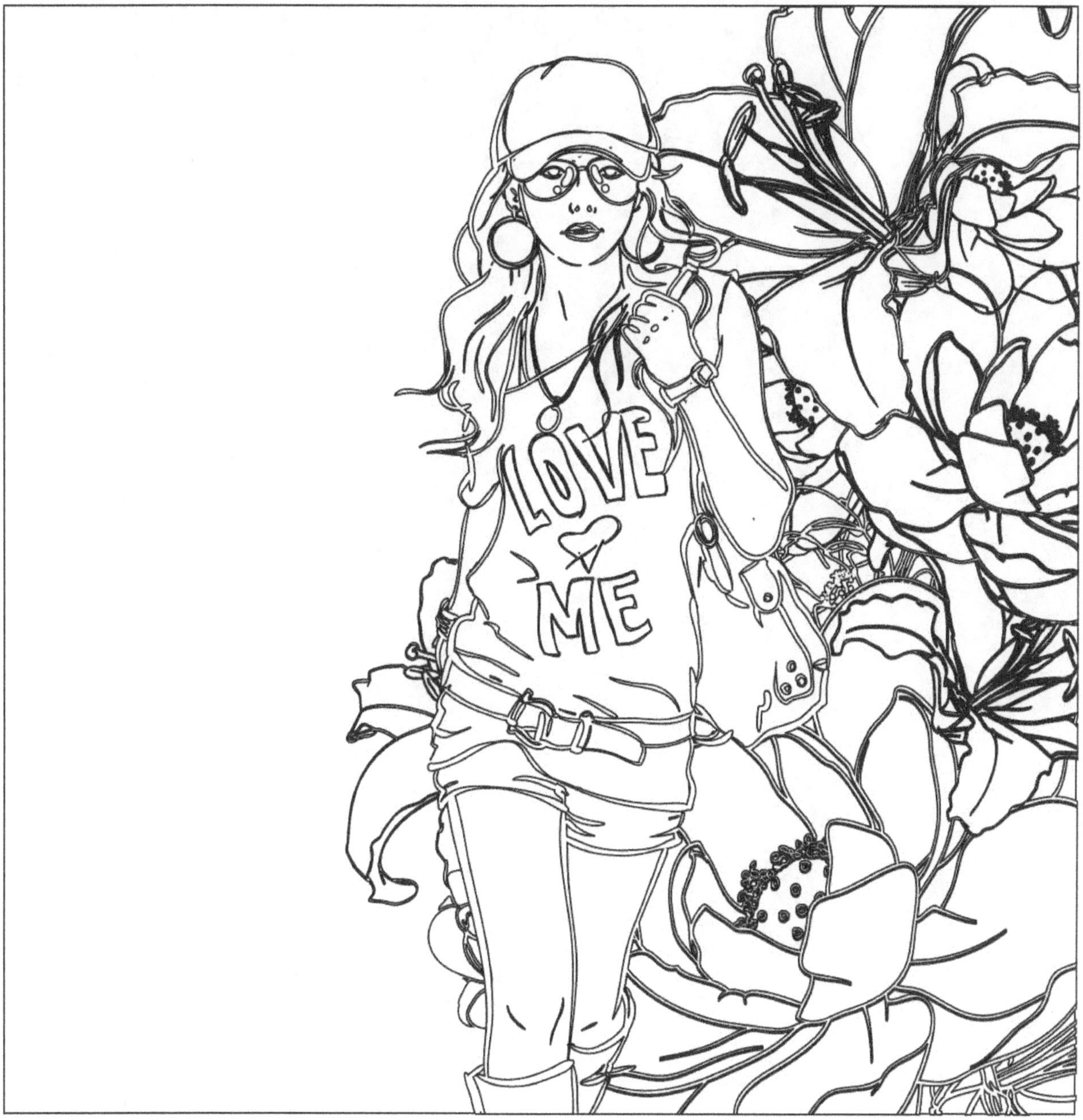
LOVE
ME

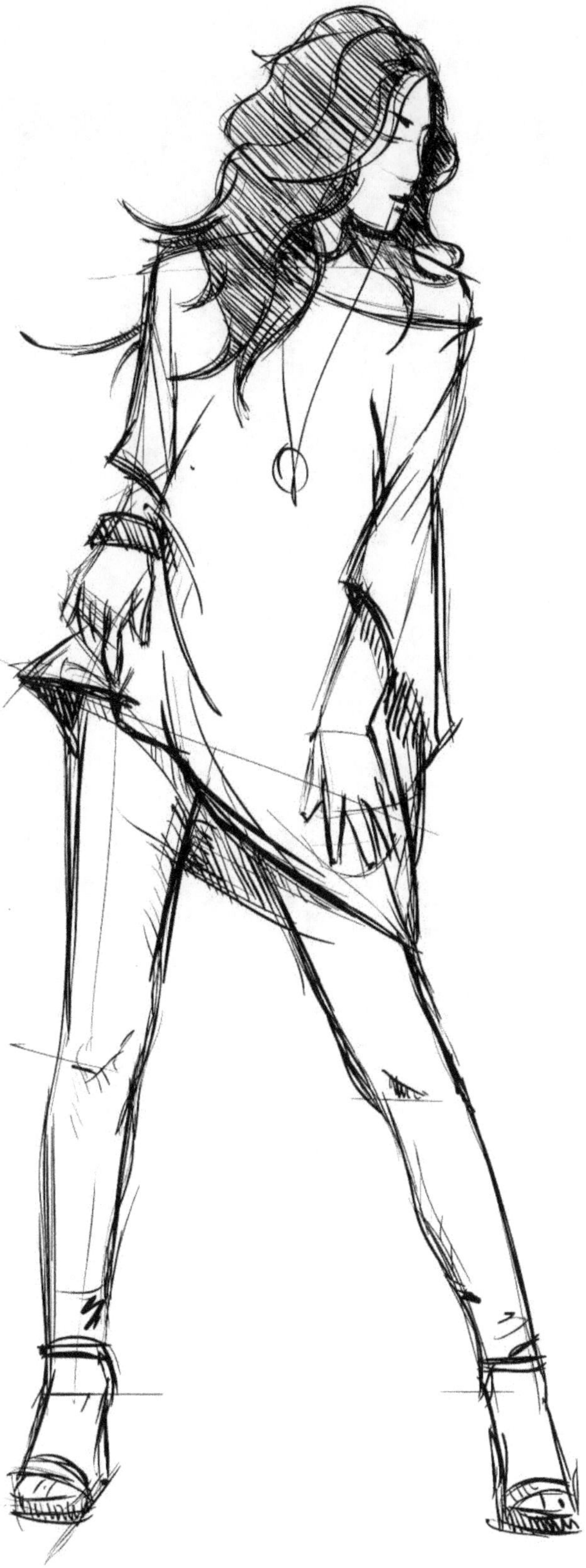

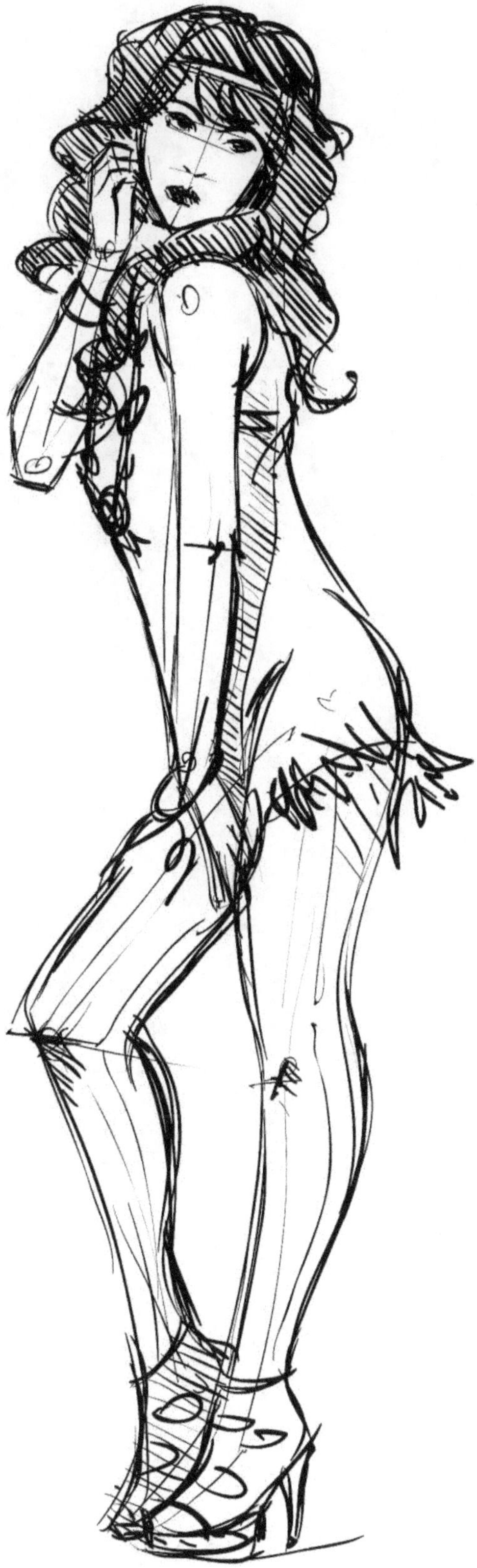

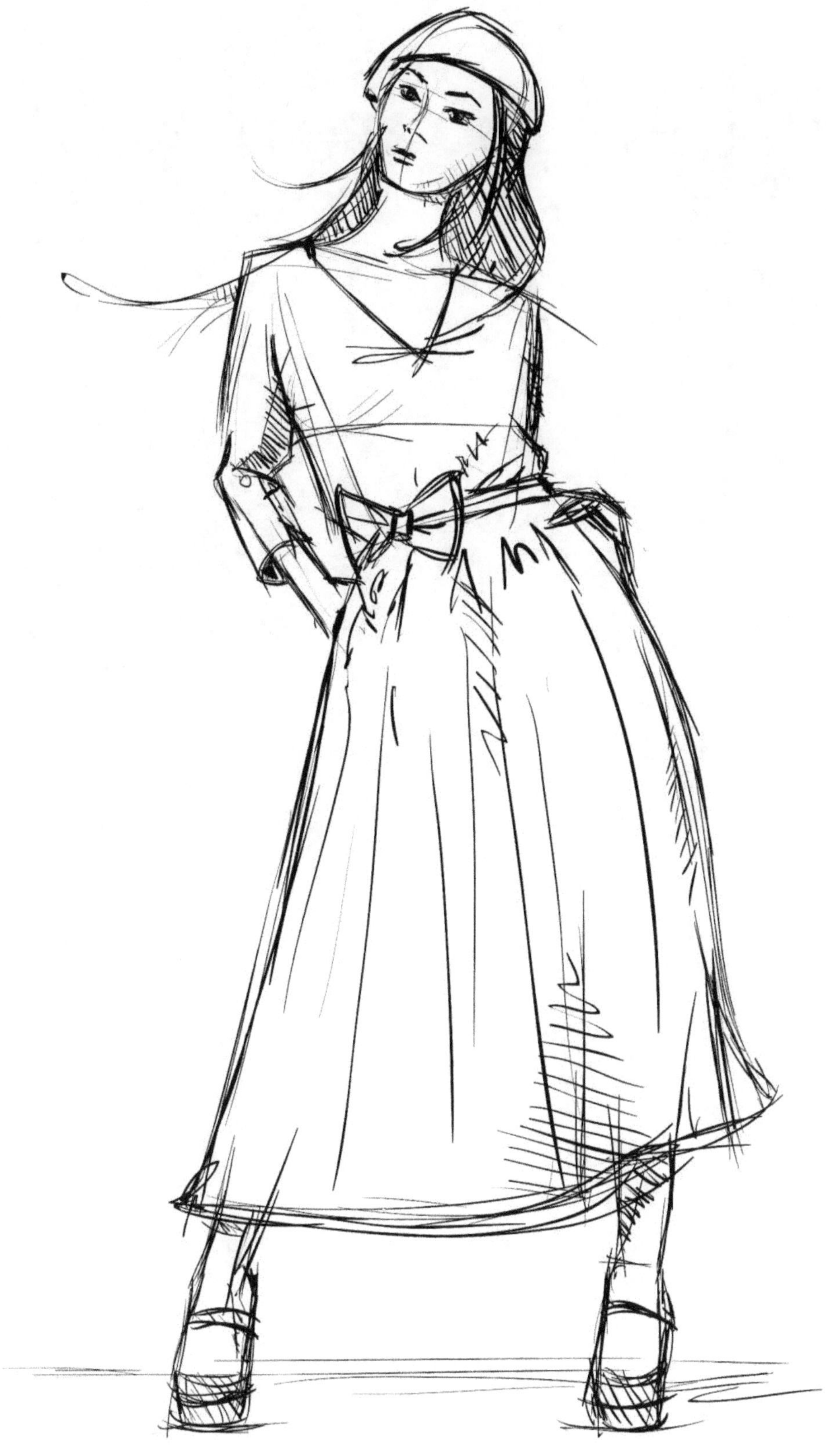

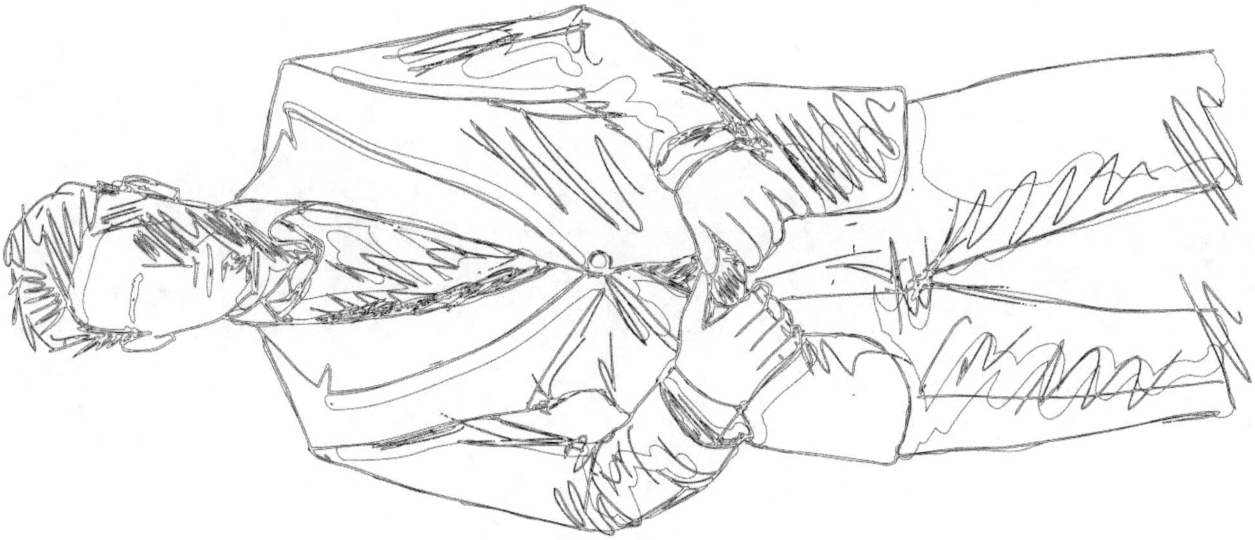
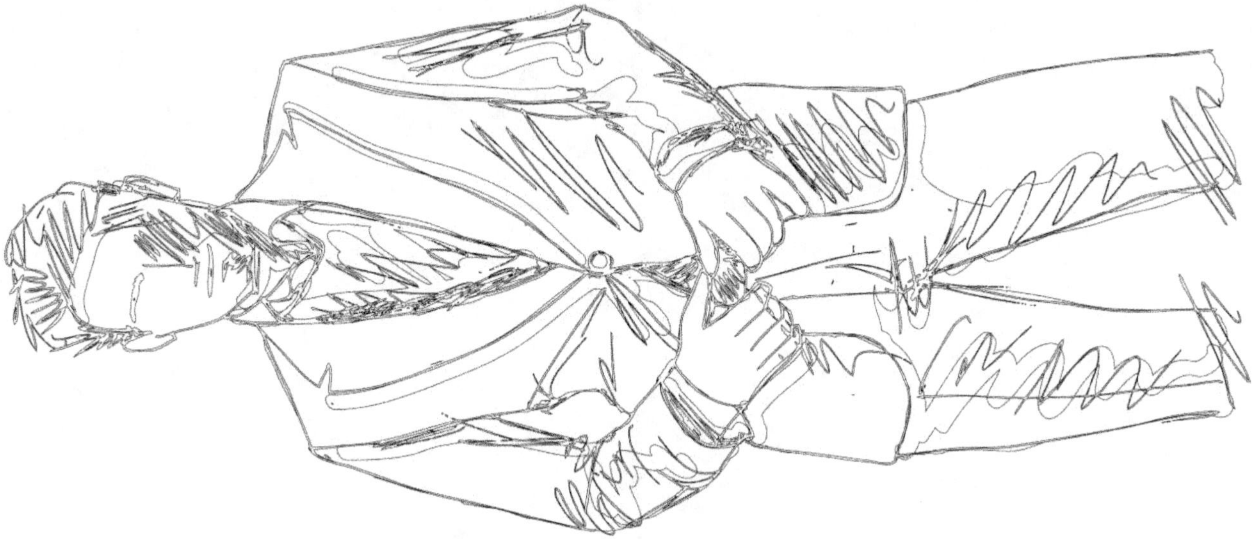
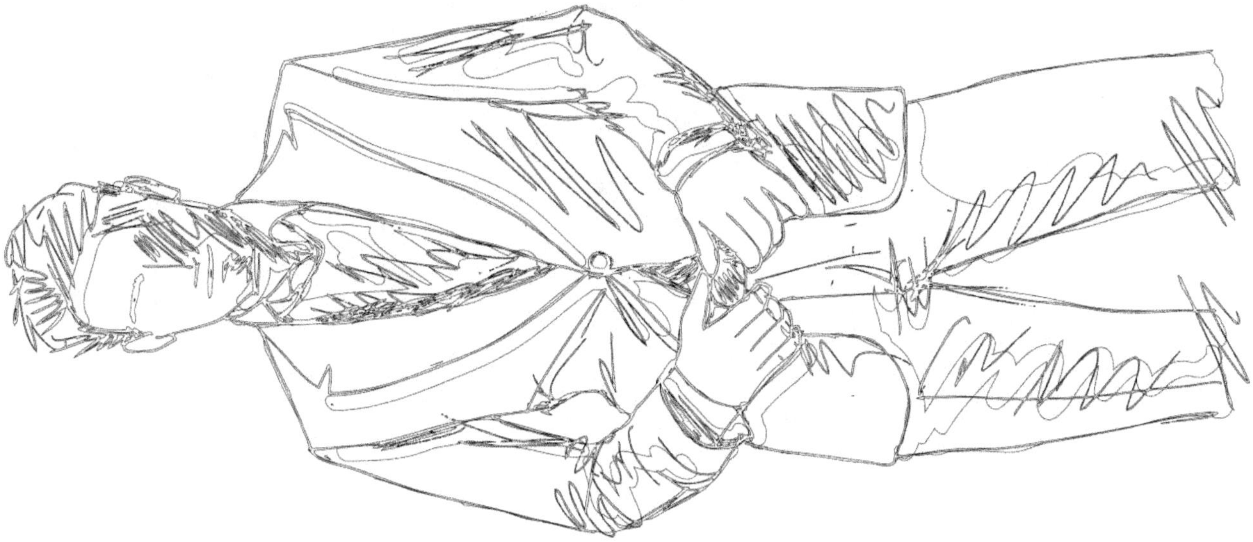

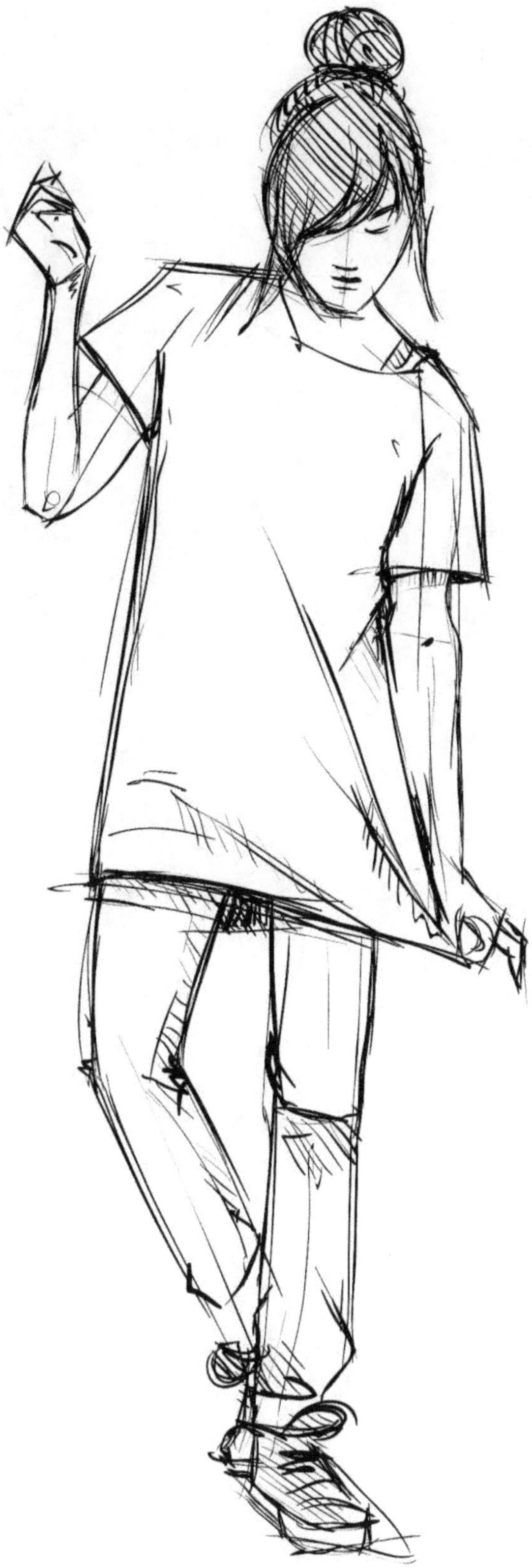

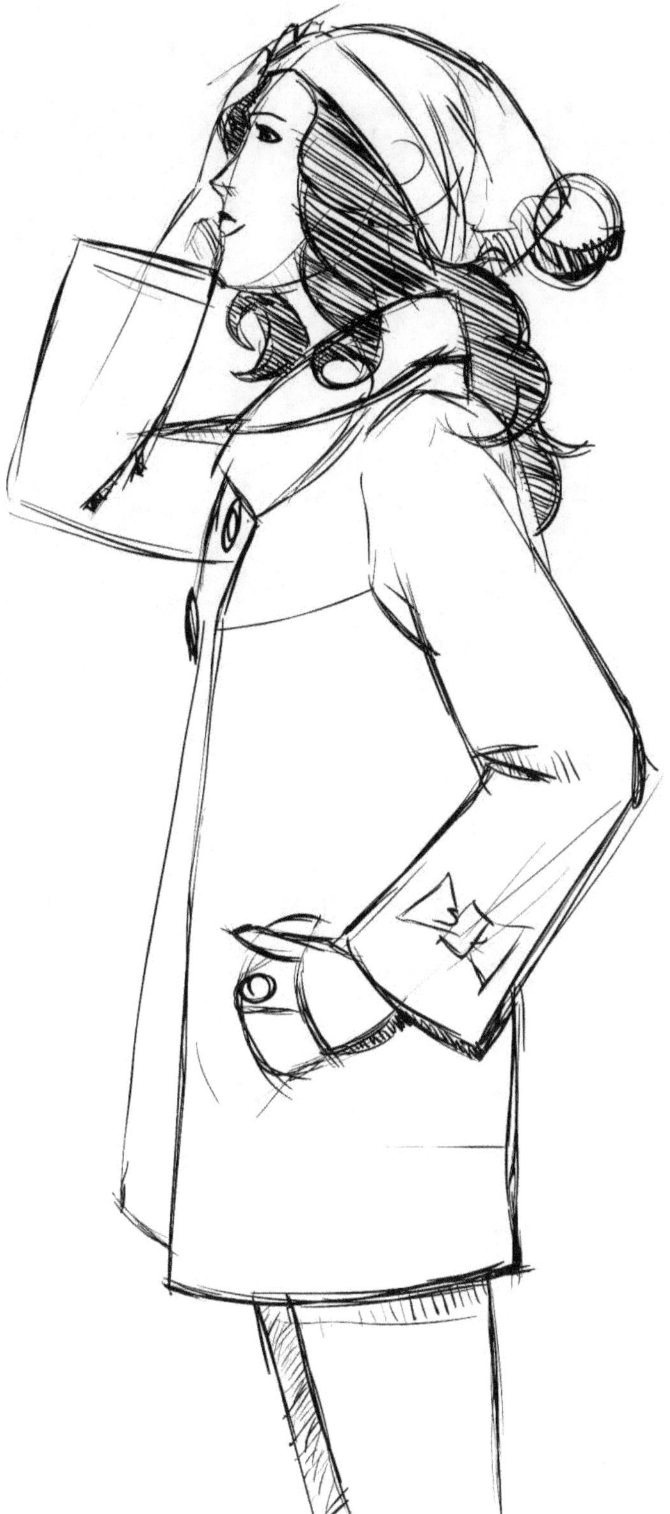

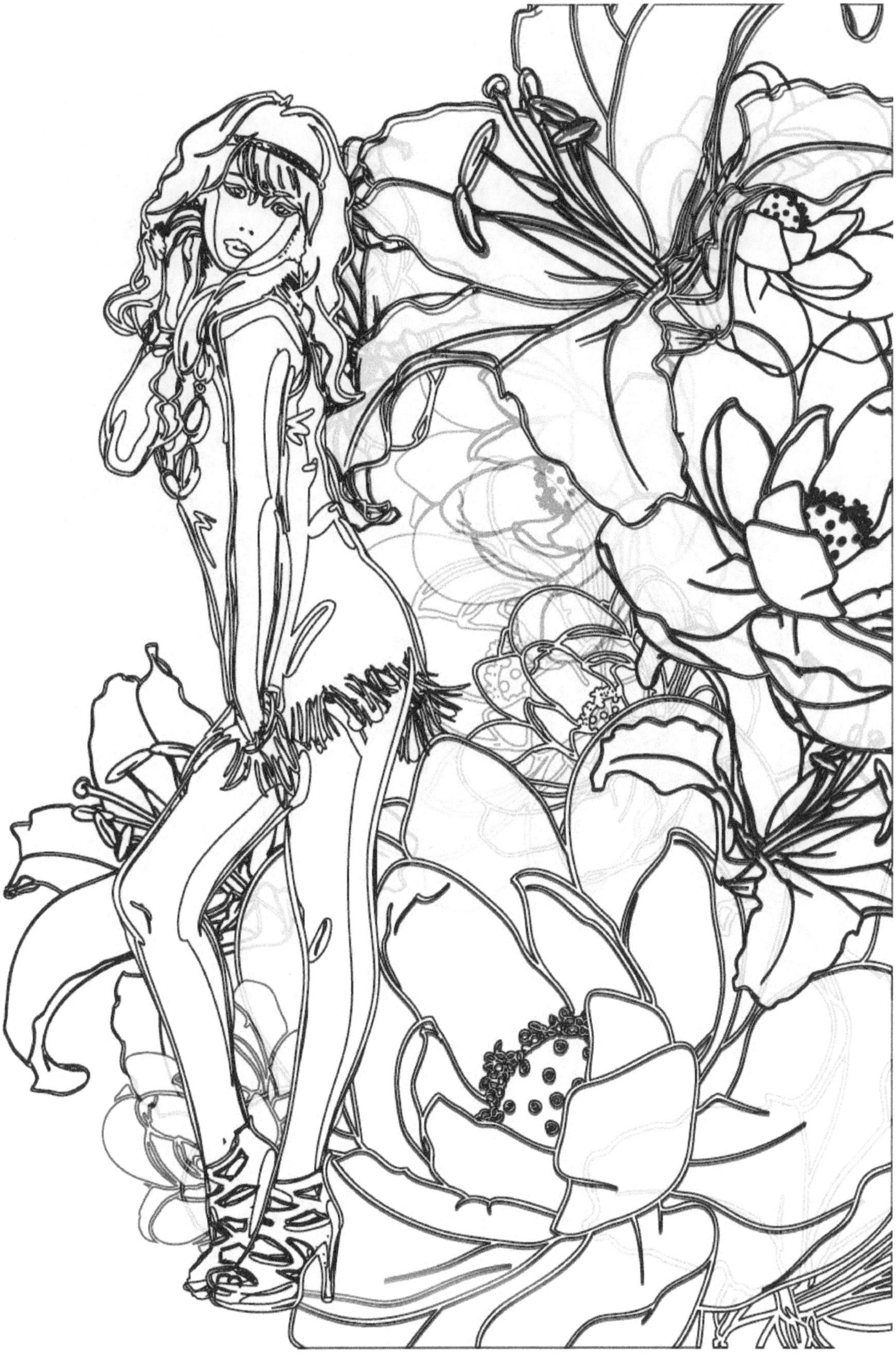

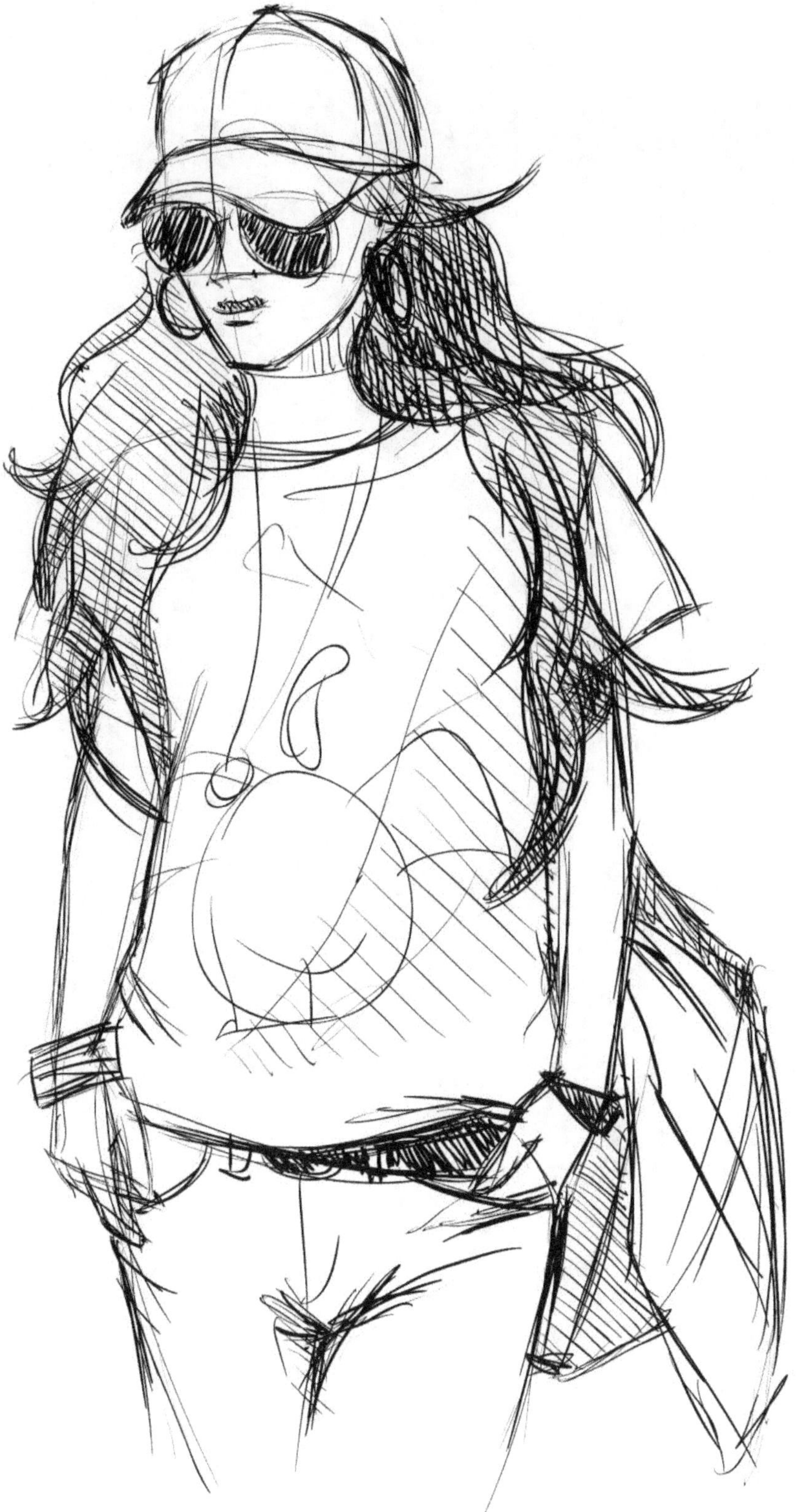

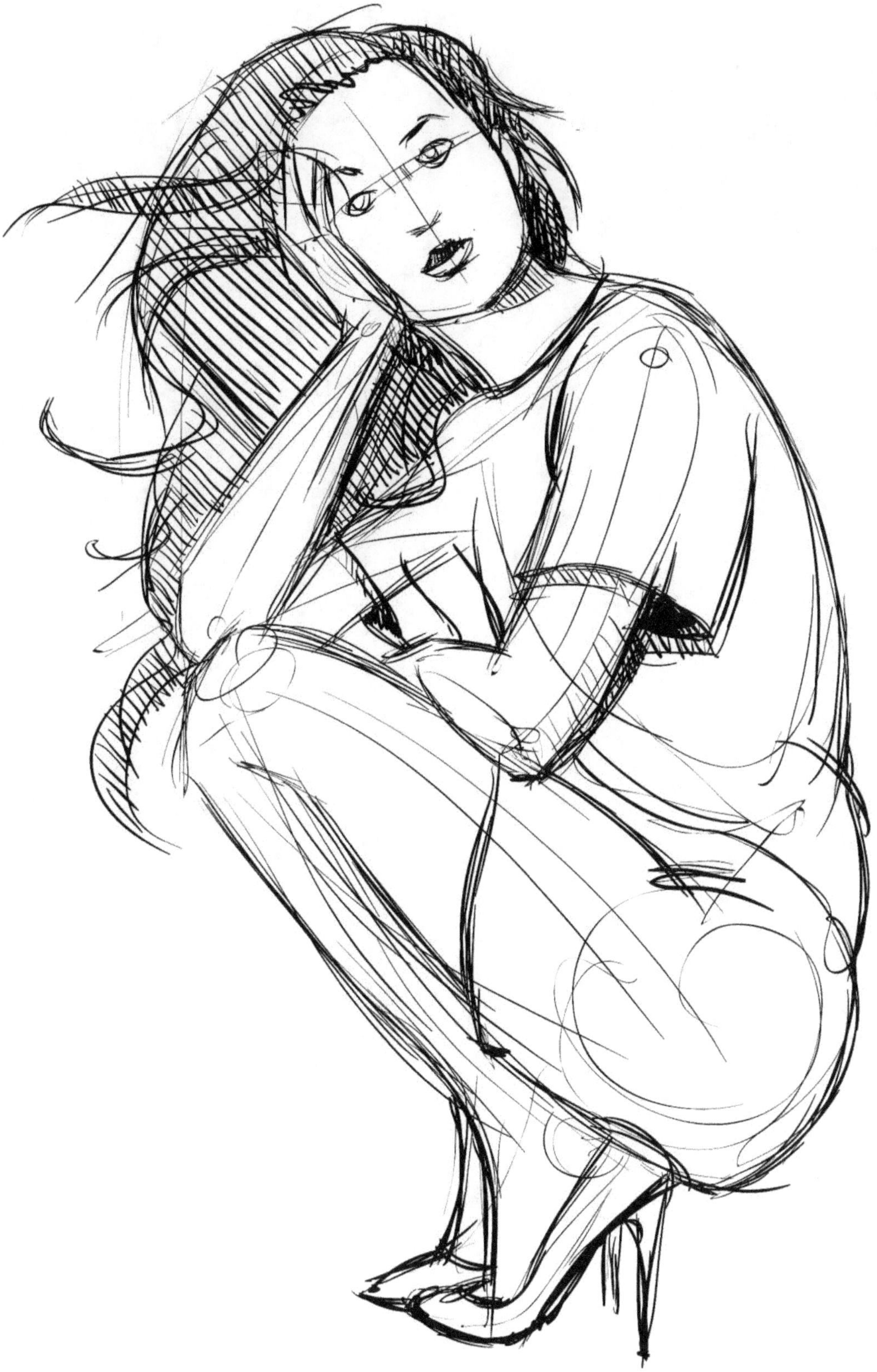

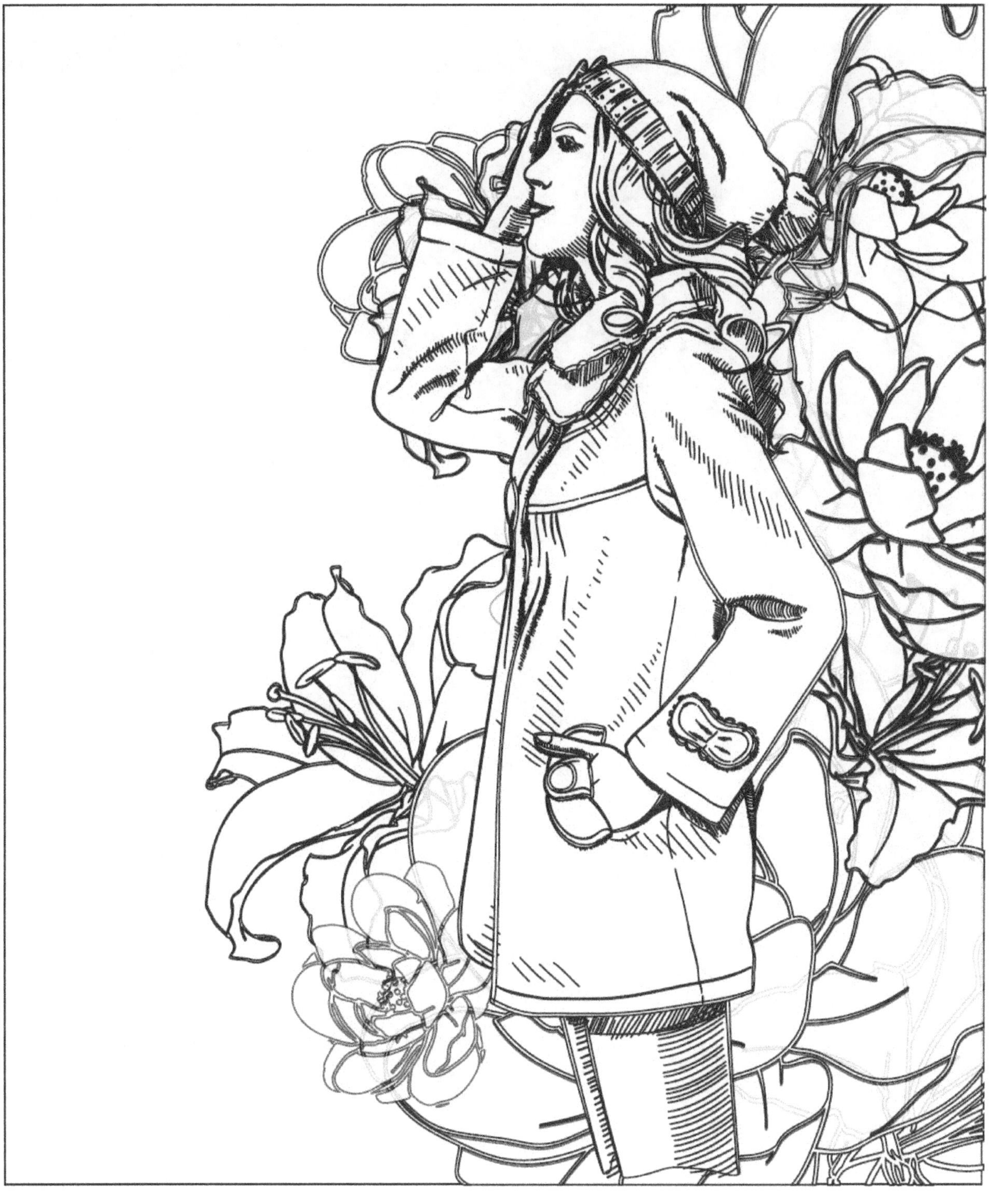

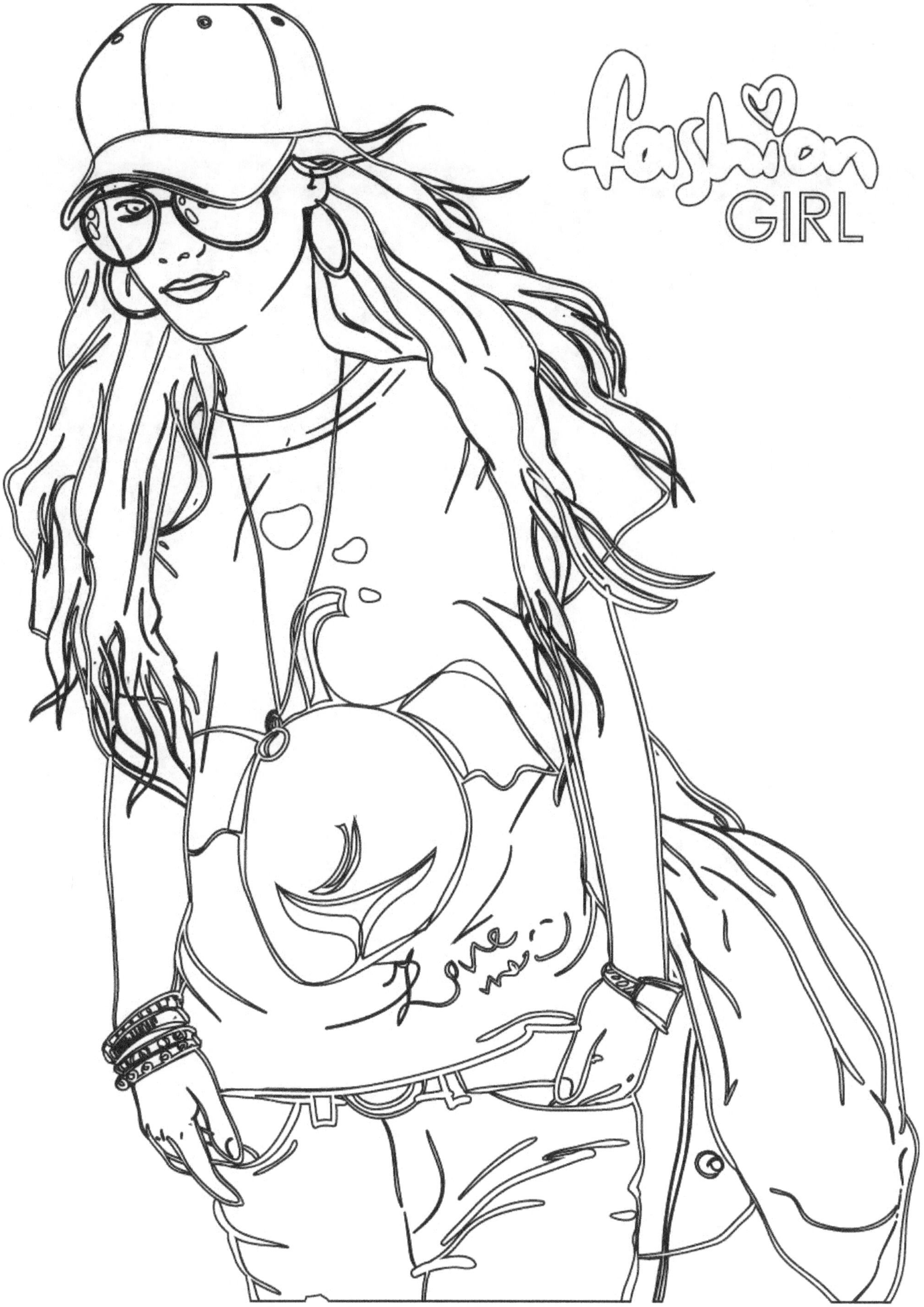
fashion
GIRL

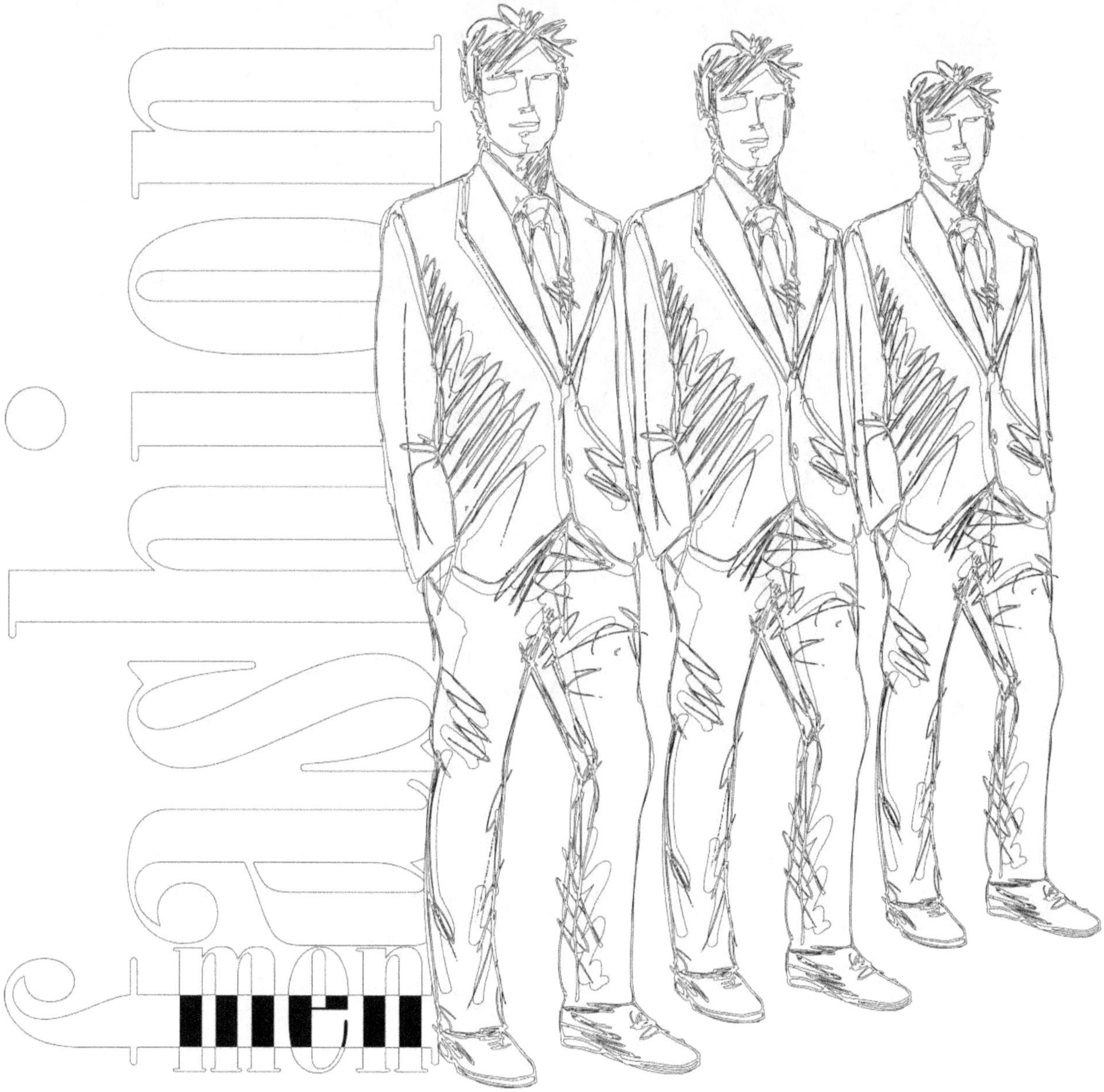
fashion
men

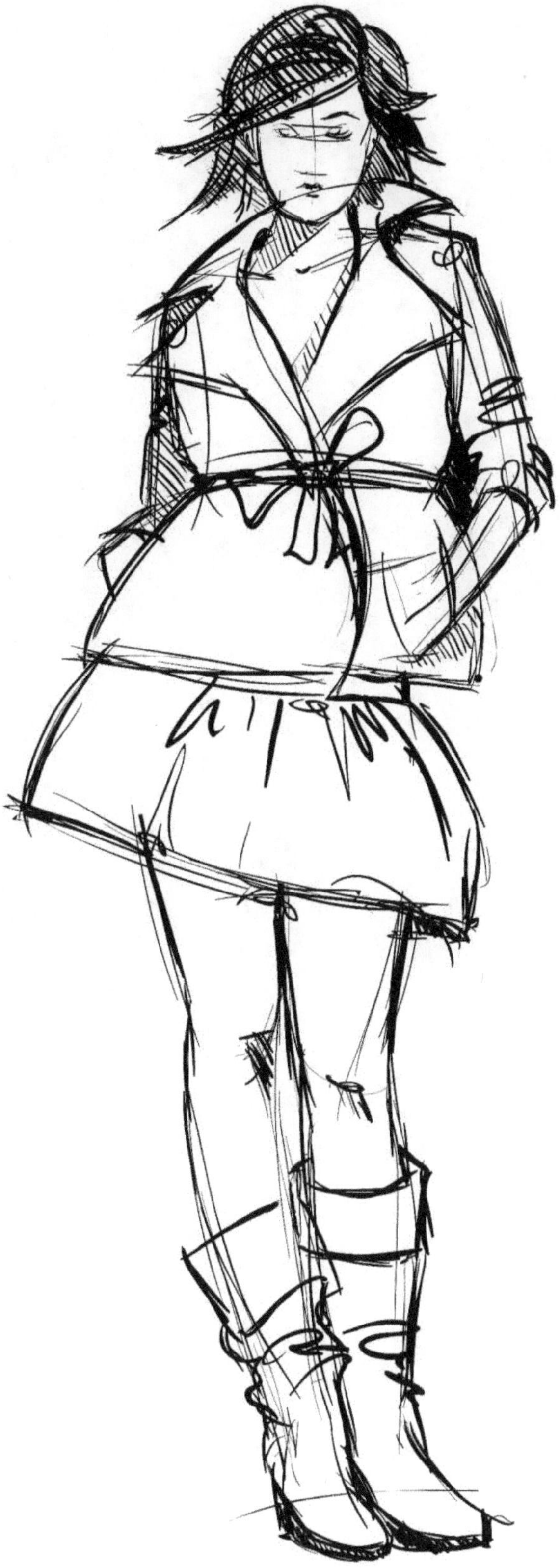

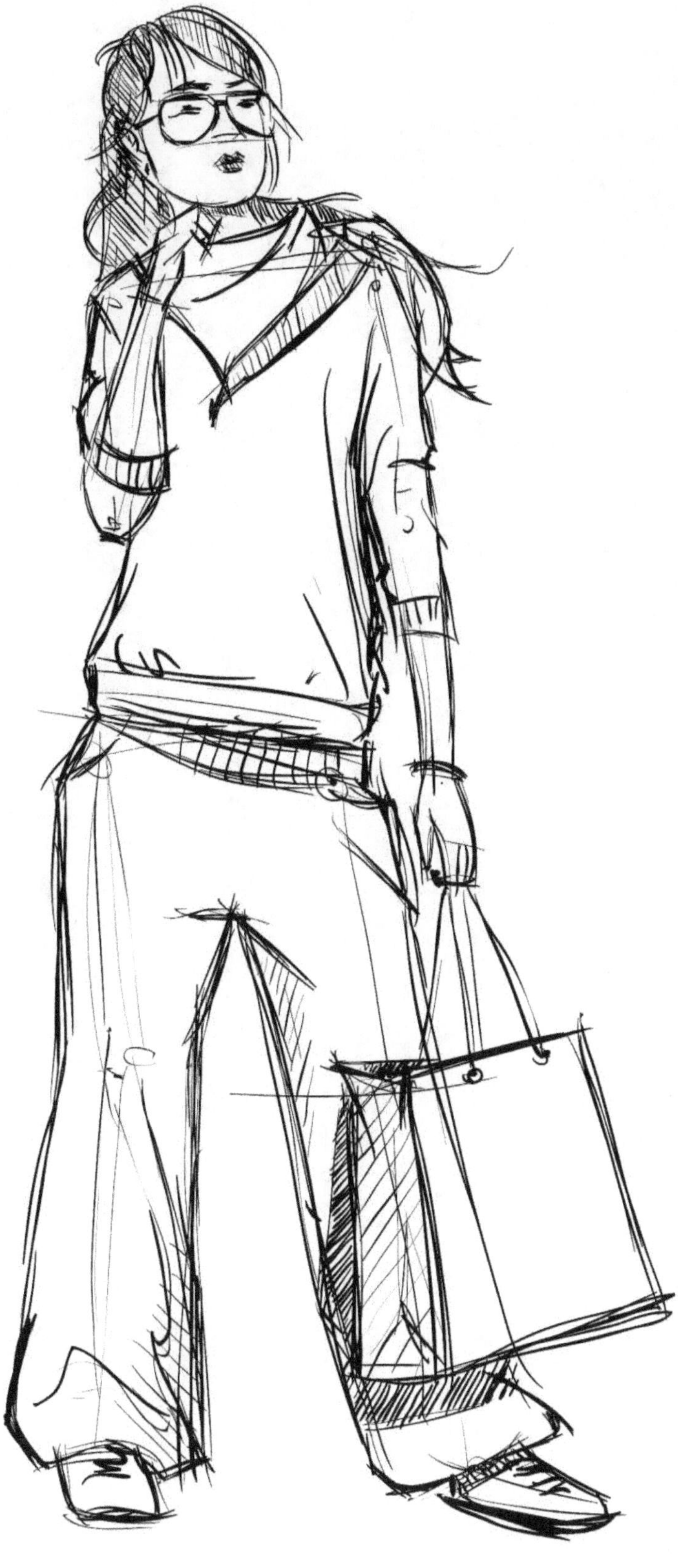

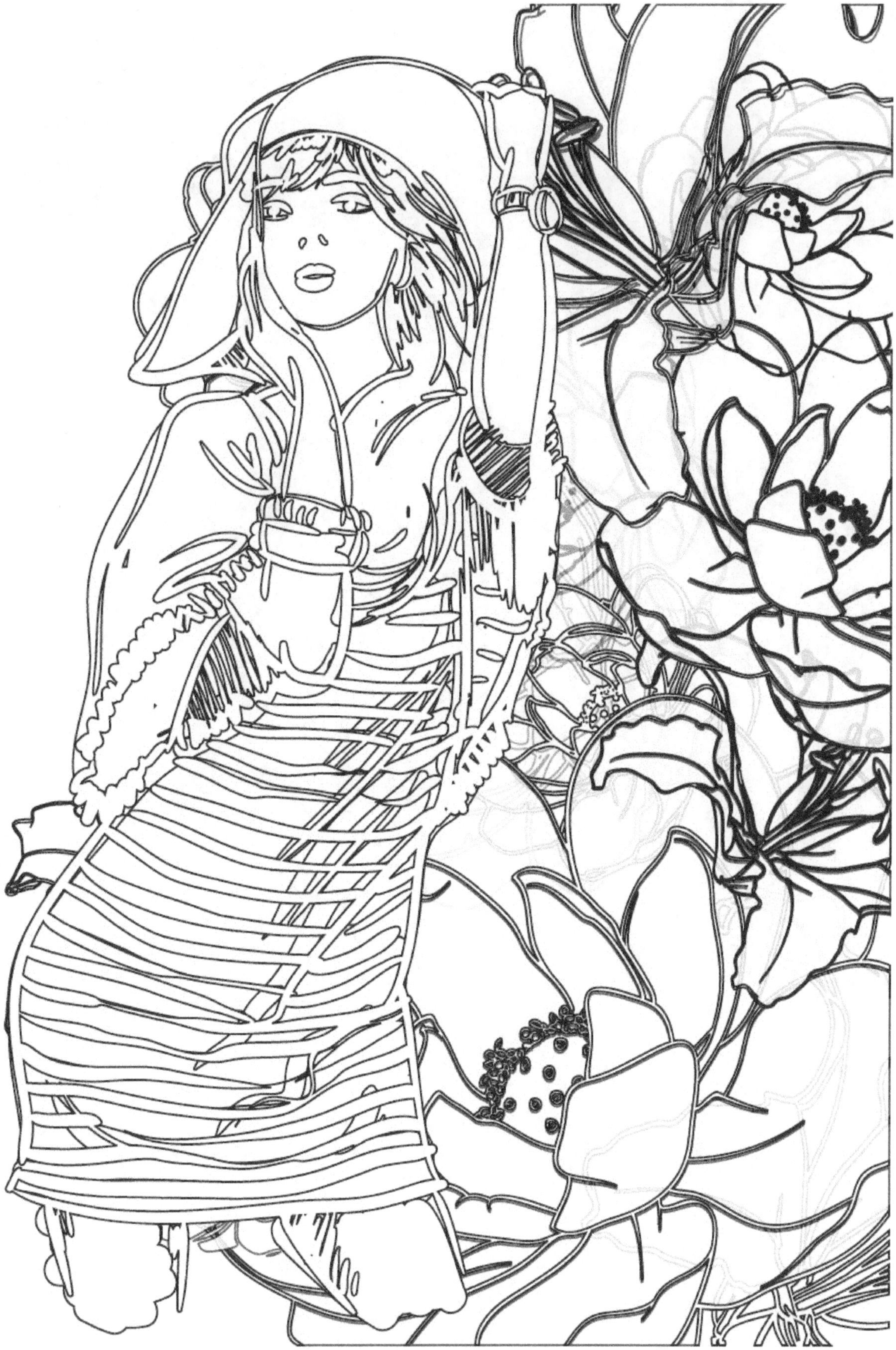

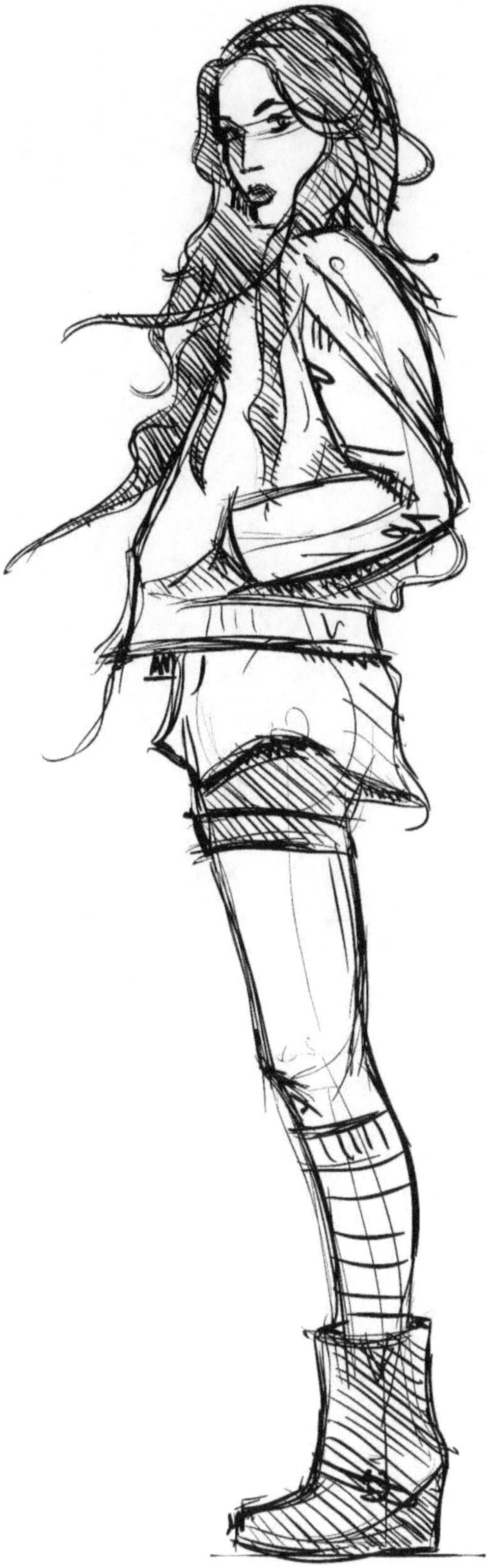

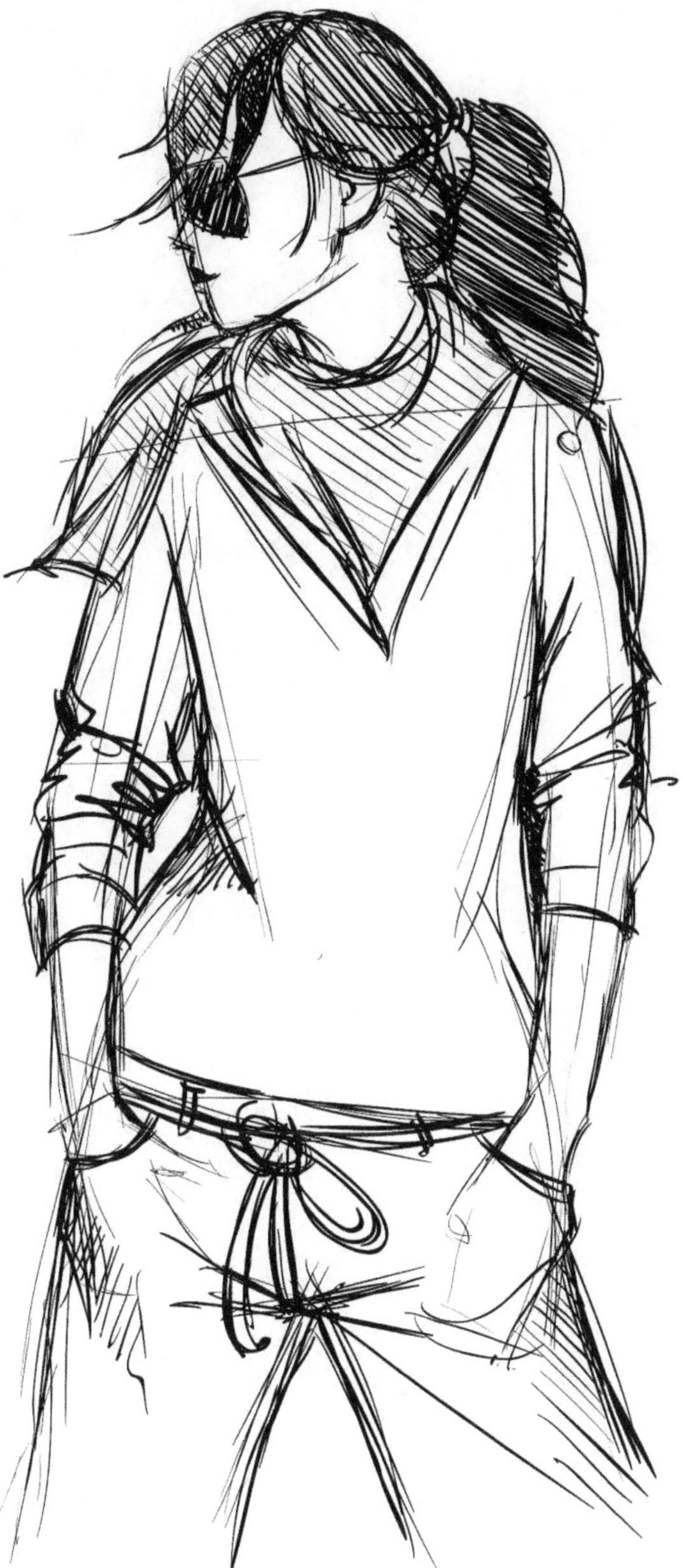

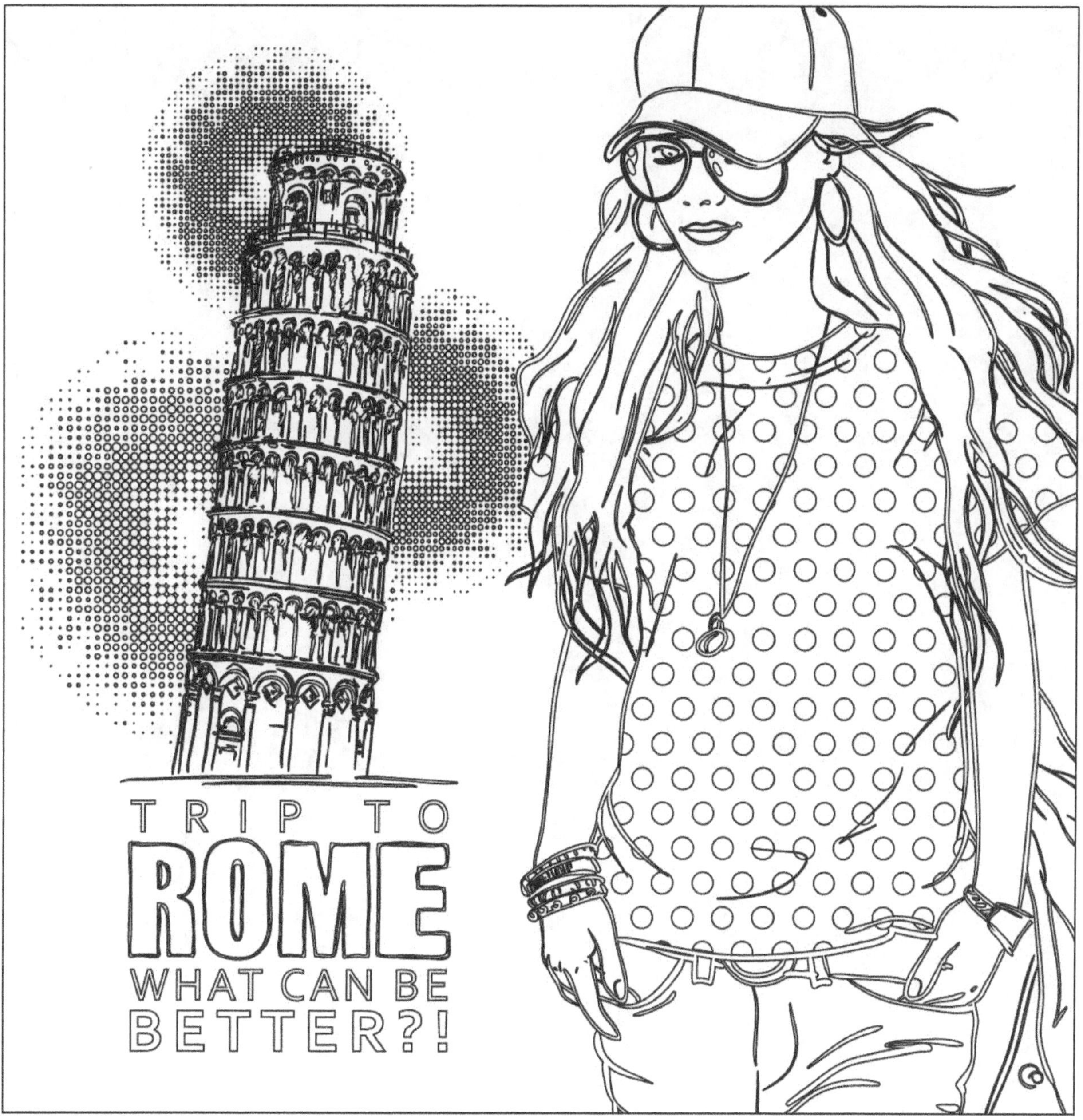
TRIP TO
ROME
WHAT CAN BE
BETTER?!

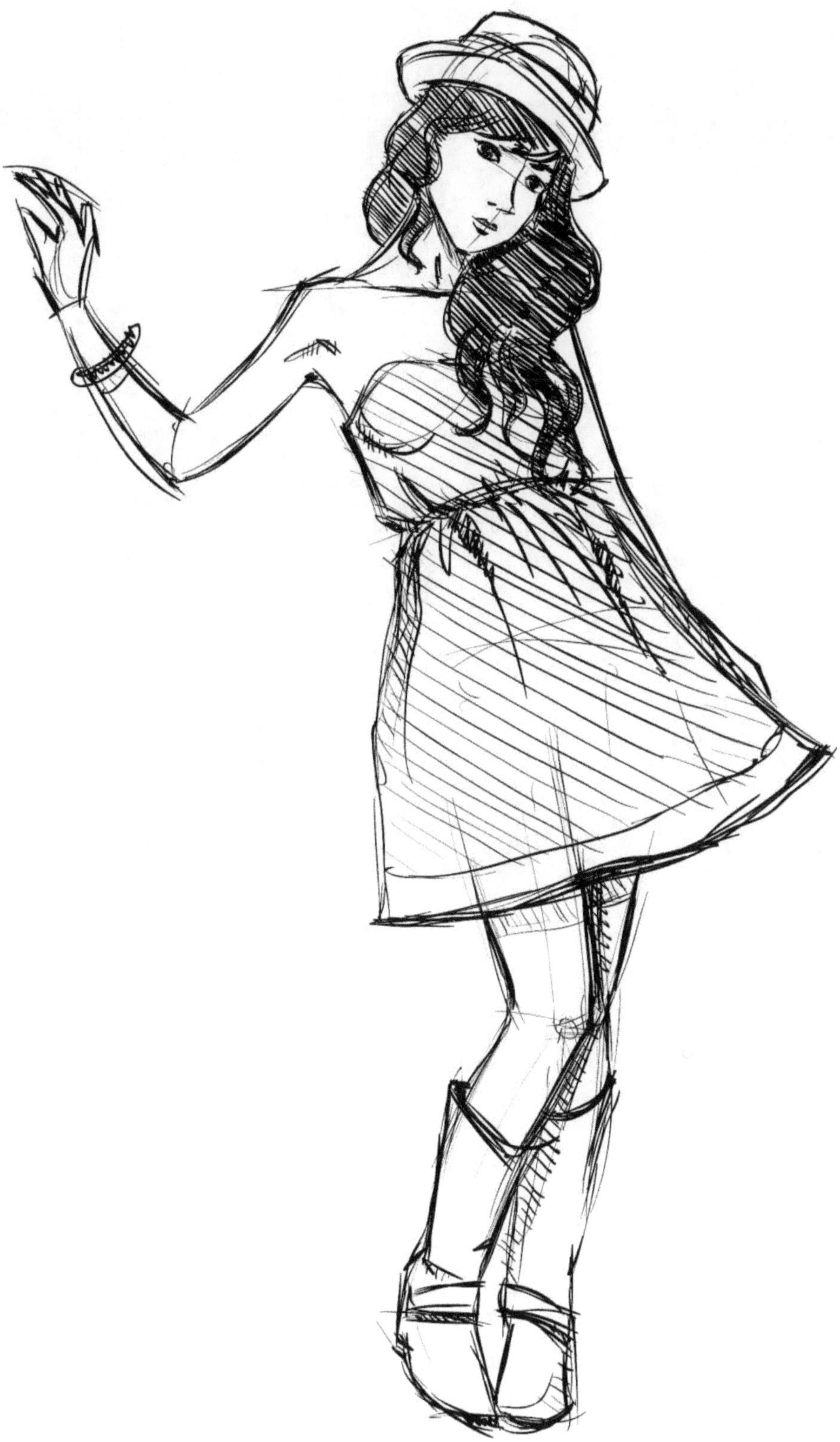

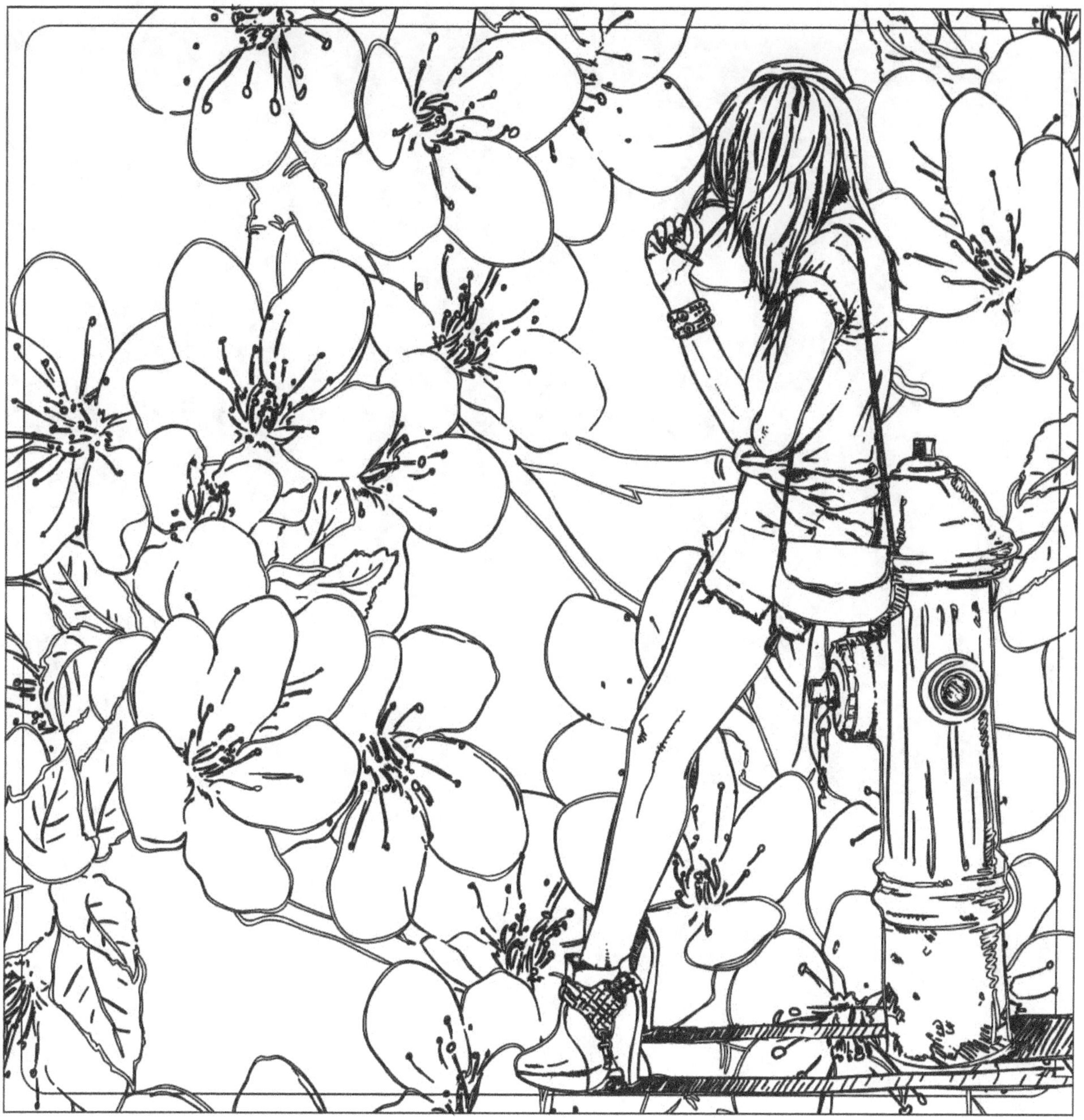

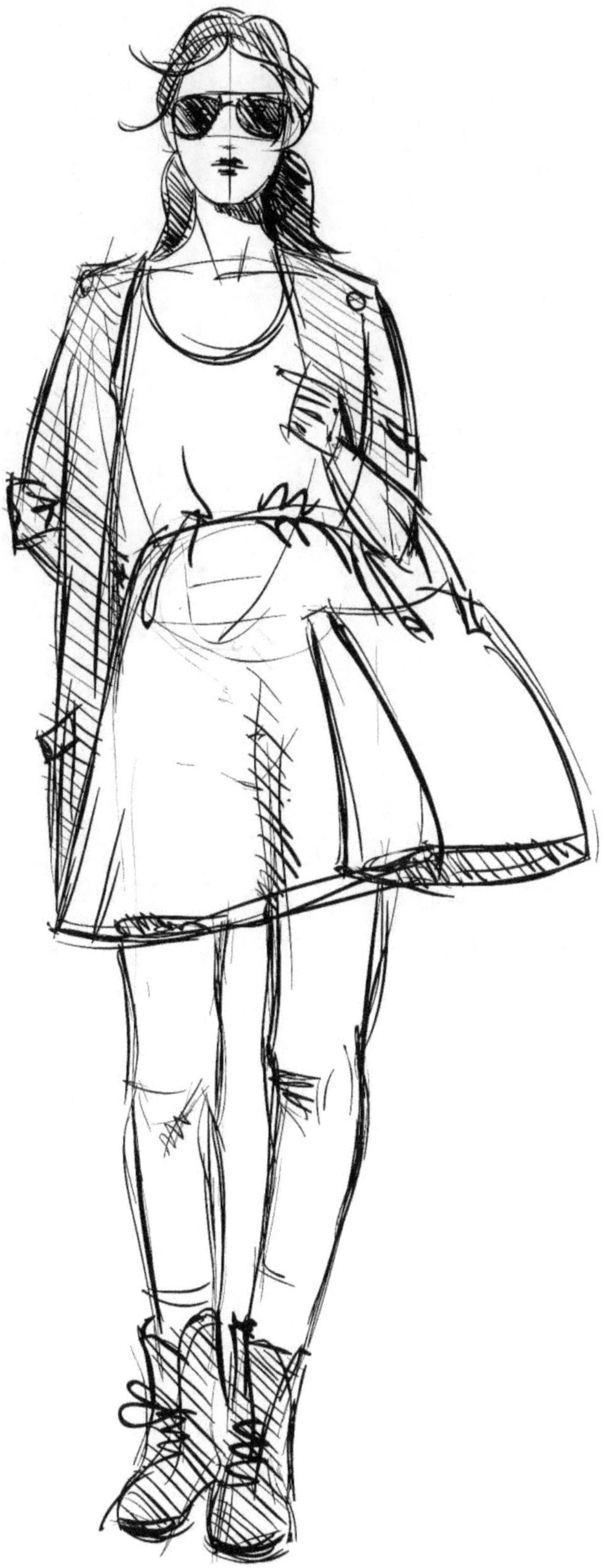

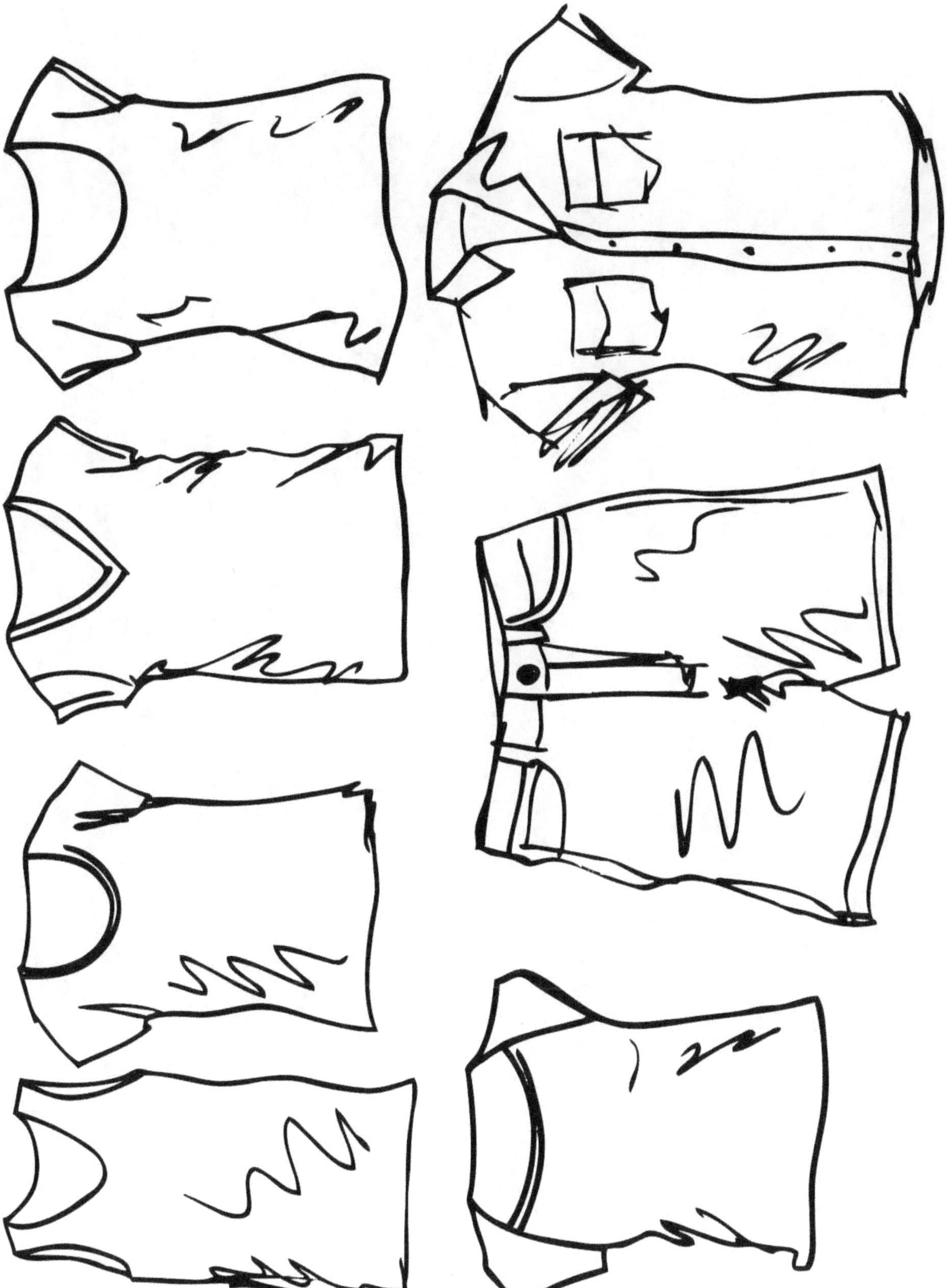

www.ingramcontent.com/pod-product-compliance
Lightning Source LLC
Chambersburg PA
CBHW080544190526
45169CB00007B/2634